Living
In
Eternity

Efrosini A. Pappas

BALBOA
PRESS
A DIVISION OF HAY HOUSE

Copyright © 2018 Efrosini A. Pappas.

All rights reserved. No part of this book may be used or reproduced by any means, graphic, electronic, or mechanical, including photocopying, recording, taping or by any information storage retrieval system without the written permission of the author except in the case of brief quotations embodied in critical articles and reviews.

Cover : "Eternity" watercolor by Efrosini

Balboa Press books may be ordered through booksellers or by contacting:

Balboa Press
A Division of Hay House
1663 Liberty Drive
Bloomington, IN 47403
www.balboapress.com
1 (877) 407-4847

Print information available on the last page.

ISBN: 978-1-9822-0869-1 (sc)
ISBN: 978-1-9822-0870-7 (e)

Efrosini A. Pappas
310/600-2870
efrosini5@gmail.com

Balboa Press rev. date: 11/27/2018

CONTENTS

Preface ix
    A Simple Life Changing Experience

Chapter 1. 1
    Appearances Of Happiness

Chapter 2. 5
    The Layers Of Logic

Chapter 3. 9
    One Heart

Chapter 4. 13
    The Unexplainable

Chapter 5. 17
    Discovering My Universe

Chapter 6. 21
    Time Travel

Chapter 7. 25
    Surviving

Chapter 8. 31
    Forever Present

Chapter 9. 35
    Angels On Earth

Chapter 10. 39
    Understanding My Reality

Chapter 11. 43
    Learning From My Parents

Chapter 12. 49
Communicating Across Boundaries
Chapter 13. 55
The Promise Of Youth
Chapter 14. 61
Dreams Or Fantasy
Chapter 15. 65
A Miracle
Chapter 16. 71
The Passing Of Time
Chapter 17. 75
Interfacing With The Spirit World
Chapter 18. 79
Walking The Labyrinth
Chapter 19. 85
Heaven On Earth
Chapter 20. 91
The Continuation Of Life
Chapter 21. 97
A New Beginning
Chapter 22. 101
A Final Goodbye
Chapter 23. 107
The Circle Of Life
Post Script 113
By The Way

*... dedicated to my loving family
without whom
my life would be meaningless...*

"To be yourself in a world that is constantly trying to make you something else is the greatest accomplishment."

Ralph Waldo Emerson

"You have a brush.
You have your color.
Paint paradise.
Then go in."

Nikos Kazantzakis

Preface
A Simple **L**ife **C**hanging Experience

Life is unpredictable. We don't know from one moment to the next when the course of our life will change.

Have you ever felt there was something you've been waiting to hear without knowing what it is or why? This was one of those times.

It was 2002. I was returning to the United States from Botswana, and during a layover at the Johannesburg airport, I went into the bookstore and browsed through the aisles. I was intrigued by the title of a book, *The Miracle of Mindfulness,* written by Thich Nhat Hahn, a Buddhist monk exiled from Vietnam. I perused it, bought it, and never regretted it. The book so profoundly resonated with me that it unconsciously set me on a path I had never envisioned.

Can that be described as a meaningful experience? Was it coincidental? I don't believe in meaningless occurrences. I believe there are clues that come to us when the time is right, the time to address issues in our life, and this was one of them.

Let me go back in time. Shortly after the birth of my second son in 1966, my life changed. It became apparent to me that my experiences may be worth sharing. It wasn't easy. I had to first learn to set aside the limitations imposed upon me by a society that knew as little as I. As I began to look at the events in my life with an expanded vision, my life took on new perspectives. I believed in what I was about to write, but no matter how hard I tried, I couldn't.

When my son died in 1981 I was determined to write about what led me to this place in my journey. However, things don't happen when we want them to happen; they happen when they're meant to happen. It was despair over my daughter-in-law's death in 2000 that finally enabled me to begin to sort out my thoughts and feelings.

Not knowing if I had a message, I took a leap of faith and began writing vignettes of personal stories, mine and others. My book became a long work-in-progress as I tried to process everything so that even *I* could understand.

You are now about to read what took place over a period of 50+ years that changed the way I looked at and lived my life. *Living In Eternity* is written as a narrative woven with glimpses of visionary experiences, which I hope you will read with your heart.

It is a story about grief, longing, searching, about prayer, love, miracles, and life-changing events ... a story which may parallel yours. The chapters are presented in an unplanned manner, however, I hope I have made it possible for you to find a connecting thread between them and follow my stream of consciousness.

It isn't religious or scientific, however, it does include both, written by someone who is not an authority on either. I make mention of children - I have been blessed with five; and grandchildren - I have twelve. Names have been omitted to protect their privacy.

The pronoun 'I' is used to signify everything I have personally experienced and/or perceived to have experienced, knowing that others may view them differently through their own perspectives. For those shared by others, I use the pronouns 'he' and 'she.' They are real to them and a private part of themselves and their memories, and that's all that matters. I have set these personal experiences apart from my narrative in an italic format to convey the moments of clarity that pierce the veil of time.

Often there is one individual who unknowingly sets us on an alternative journey. For me, it was my cousin who led me off the beaten path. It was he who opened my third eye, an invisible inner eye providing me with a perception beyond ordinary sight to all possibilities, and to whom I offer my gratitude and love.

What I have learned is minuscule when measured by the span of eternal life and all there is to learn. It did, however, lead me on an inspirational journey that opened the door to a continuation of knowledge that brought me happiness and peace, one which may not have otherwise been part of my present reality. It also reinforced my belief that there is no separation of time between the past, present, and future. There is only now; Eternity; and my book took life.

Standing in one spot, we see one picture, a picture that has multiple angles, one that has infinite possibilities. Each time we make a choice, we create another reality. Some of our choices don't seem to be important at the time, or appropriate, but they shape our lives.

You bought this book. Why have you chosen to read it? Perhaps you were intrigued by the title, the concept, or it became your time to open your third eye. How you interpret it is up to you.

"Live each moment in its entirety."

Author Unknown

Chapter One
Appearances **O**f **H**appiness

Let me start at the beginning ... one of many.

It was a hot June night. There was not a breath of fresh air; nothing stirred. Even the grass and flowers curled waiting revival, which would come with the early morning dew. Two fans were oscillating in opposite directions in the corners of the room I had occupied for the past three months. My bed now consisted of the carpet, and my pillow, the towel I would be using the following morning.

There was an uneasiness in my spirit. I had a long trip ahead of me, and I needed the sleep. Was it the heat that kept me awake or the anticipation of saying a second goodbye to a place that held precious memories that was coloring my early morning rise? As the sun crept through the window I bolted upright, feeling somehow that I was already running late. Despite the urgency, I took a long hot shower with the events of the past three months running fast forward in my mind.

It was like an April fool joke.
I didn't believe it at first when my eldest child, my first-born son, and daughter-in-law asked me to move in with them. Although we lived a five minute walk apart, we respected each other's independent lifestyles, privacy, and space. We were there for one another, but did not impose regularly planned visits or daily phone calls.

Occasionally, when my daughter-in-law ran errands in the afternoon, she would drop off my granddaughters, and I would enjoy indulging in some creative fantasy play with them. They were a bright glow in my otherwise workaholic teaching life, as I was traveling back and forth into New York, Connecticut, and Massachusetts. Needless to say, there was not much to think about. I accepted their offer.

During the next three months life criss-crossed between a roller coaster and spinning ferris wheel. My son received a once-in-a-lifetime offer in Bethesda, Maryland; my daughter-in-law announced she was pregnant with twin boys; and my daughter became engaged to be married. I was very happy. We were all looking forward with anticipation to a new wonderful adventure for each of us.

The house was placed on the market and sold in one day. For whatever reason, it was meant to be. In two weeks we were all packed up, and our lives were headed down separate roads. My son and his family were on their way to Maryland for a new beginning, stopping for a brief vacation for rest and relaxation at the Jersey shore before moving into their new home. I stayed behind to close up the house and once helping them get settled in their new home, I would be heading towards a new beginning - destination unknown.

The time had come for me to bid farewell to an area in Connecticut in which I had twice made my life. The first, for twelve years ending in 1981 with the death of my second-born son and my marriage; and the second, for seven years after returning in anticipation of the birth of my first grandchild, my granddaughter.

I packed my car and began my second goodbye – driving past the houses in which we lived; Friendly's, where we enjoyed Swiss Chocolate Almond ice cream sundaes after school functions; and the pond downtown where we fed the ducks and geese. I circled around to the schools each of my children attended, passed the library, and picked up my last cup of coffee and donut in the town in which I had lived for so many years. I was finally ready and headed for the open road.

What followed changed all our lives forever. How often we believe we are heading towards a chosen direction, and then we encounter a major fork in the road that changes destiny. When one past ends, does another future begin? When one door closes, does another one open?

Never would I have imagined there would be a twist in the road that would drag us emotionally through unbearable agony - through hell.

In his book, *Emotional Intelligence,* Daniel Goleman wrote, *'… reason without feeling is blind.'*

Steve Jobs, industrial designer, innovator, and Co-Founder of Apple, Inc., said, *'Have the courage to follow your heart and intuition.'*

Our intuition is all we have that enables us to reveal to ourselves that what we hold in our mind can connect us with our inner voice, an instinct beneath the layers of our logic. Mine evolved through love and heartbreak.

*"We are travelers on a cosmic journey...
We have stopped...to love, to share.
This precious moment is
a little parenthesis in eternity."*

Paulo Coelho

Chapter Two
The Layers Of Logic

It was a warm sunny day in August, and I was expecting my second child. The heat was unbearable. I had just left the doctor's office where I was told my baby was too content to make an entry into the world. But my instinct told me differently. It was my body, and I knew what I was feeling. This little baby was definitely ready and eager to make an entrance into this life.

I felt such joy in anticipation of the birth of my second child. I wanted a sibling for my first born son as much as he did. We spent the day together playing and making plans for his approaching 4th birthday, while eagerly awaiting the birth of his sibling. Although I prepared dinner, I couldn't eat. Once putting my son to bed, I told my husband it was time to leave for the hospital, and in a couple of hours my smiling Irishman was born.

No, we're not Irish, but he had that red ruddy Irish complexion. He kept smiling as he slept and looked happy and peaceful; a quiet newborn, too quiet, which perhaps should have been an indication that something was not quite right. I dismissed the feeling. My son was released from the hospital as a healthy baby; being quiet didn't necessarily mean that something was wrong, did it?

The inner voice within me kept nagging at me. I couldn't rid myself of a strong sense that something was not quite right. I won't go into the details of the next couple of days except to say that had I not heeded my intuition, I would not have this story to tell.

I insisted that our pediatrician see him, rejecting his advice that I stop worrying because young mothers overreact and should remain calm. There is no such thing as overreacting when your baby appears to be in distress, his life being threatened, and the possibility of his death choking you.

My son was admitted into the Emergency Room and diagnosed with heart failure brought about by the closing of the hole between the chambers of his heart. The closing of this hole is a normal process, except my son had an undetected cardiac anomaly, a three-chambered heart on the right side of his chest cavity, which upon the closing of the hole would lead to his death.

My heart quickened. I saw circles of color spiraling me downward into a black hole. I was devastated. This couldn't be true. I had entrusted my baby's well-being to the doctor. How was this possible?

Our pediatrician was faced with the most difficult task he had ever encountered … to apologize for missing the diagnosis of this rare anomaly and to tell me that my five-day old baby was not expected to live till morning.

I spent most of the night agonizing over what I should do and could do. I wasn't going to accept this fatal diagnosis. This valiant little warrior fought to come into this life, and I was *not* going to let him die. Not *my* son. I was his mother. I could not, would not, let this happen. I made phone call after phone call seeking direction. I prayed to God and cannot believe I told Him quite emphatically, in no uncertain terms, that not only wasn't I prepared, but I wasn't willing to give up my son, and I knew my son wasn't willing to leave this life before he had a chance to live it.

Eventually I reached the father of one of my students who was a cardiologist and sought his advice. Arrangements were made and in the morning, having lived through the night against all odds, my son and I were transported in an ambulance across state lines to a major hospital for babies in New York City.

Within a few days my son underwent the very first balloon catheter on a baby that young. The procedure enabled the hole between the chambers of his heart to remain open for a couple of weeks, long enough for the hospital to properly staff and prepare the team that would attempt to perform the innovative surgical procedure of keeping the hole from closing on someone that young, and my son was spared.

So often in those moments of need we find ourselves praying … to what … to whom? Does our prayer get heard? It's something that most people do automatically. That's what I did; not knowing how or why, to what or to whom, or even if my prayer would be heard. Everyone, family, friends, strangers prayed for this little baby.

This moment in time, difficult as it may be for some to understand or accept, became my first lesson in the power of prayer. Somehow through this mass prayer everyone's energy connected with and through a higher power in the universe, and my baby was given a chance to live. The impact of this mass prayer was profound. Our prayers were heard.

I did not falter in following my intuition. Because I believed in what I was feeling leads us to another beginning, one in which his smile would permeate our hearts and never falter, one in which he had to be strong enough to compensate for what he would be missing. He had to learn to understand why many of his special moments throughout his young years would be compromised. But I'm getting ahead of myself; I had to take it one day at a time.

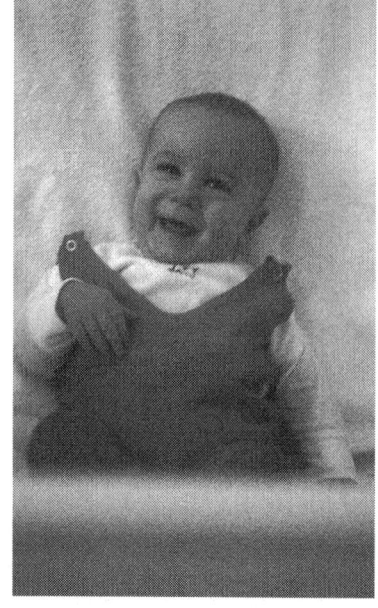

...my eye and God's eye are one eye, one seeing, one knowing, one love."

Meister Eckhart

Chapter Three
One Heart

Is there a hell? If there is, where is it? The anguish I was feeling tormented me. I felt as if I was living in a pit of despair. This has to be hell, I thought; then where is heaven? How long before I can reach eternity … before I can feel at peace? I was looking for some divine intervention that would make things right again and make this pain in my heart go away.

I had always been searching for something, somewhere, that would make me feel loved, secure ... that would give some meaning to my life. What was that something? Where was somewhere? I had often heard that my heart, the most central part of my core, is where my home is. But my heart was splintered. Things seemed hopeless. I so needed to find that place now more than ever to find some meaning to the agony I was feeling.

Meditation was new to me in those early years, however, I hoped it would help me find some peace and bring joy back into my life. I needed to feel happy again; I wanted to be happy again, however, my biggest obstacle to reaching this awareness was my mind. One day I visualized a simple phenomenon that made me realize I already had what I was seeking.

I was reflecting on what it means to really be happy, to feel peace and love. Lying down at the time, uneasy and restless, I was about to give up when I suddenly felt myself light and free, as if loftily floating through clouds. My heart began to beat quickly and heavily, sounding like a loud echo emanating from somewhere else. I placed my hand on my chest, on my heart which was beating in quick time, to assure myself that I wasn't in any tachycardia and saw a light come into my line of vision surrounding an image that was moving directly above me.

I was - perplexed. I guess that's the best way to describe how I felt because what I saw was a heart; another heart, not mine, which positioned itself upon my heart and merged into one. It was not a pulsating heart, nor an actual anatomic heart. It was clearly a valentine heart signifying love. I felt engulfed in the light. I felt comforted, and I felt loved.

Without a moment's hesitation I knew this light could only have come to me through some kind of energy from a higher power. Is that what God is ... spiritual energy? This made me realize that what I was seeking was already within me; I just didn't know it ... a heart within a heart; one within me. The knowledge was comforting; exactly what I needed.

I never really thought of words such as Light, Spirit, Energy. When I was young I prayed to someone called God. Believing what I had been taught, I didn't question His existence, nor the meaning I thought I could understand, which was that God was a higher power, all knowing and all loving, a power apart from me, not within me. It was only to Him I prayed, a prayer between Him and me, not to any interceder. As a child my God wasn't a man with a beard; I never had a visual. Simply, he always existed somewhere out there. He was just ... God.

Our scientific culture makes us focus on the physical material world, and the spiritual and holy are becoming less and less a part of our human experience ... until we face tragedy. That's when we seem to turn to prayer. To whom or to what do we pray?

It's not possible for all the people in the world to have the same religion, however, it is important to respect one another's beliefs. If people substituted a different word, such as Zeus, Allah, Source, Spirit, one that fit their personal belief for the word God, wouldn't their prayers still be one and the same? Wouldn't their religions still lead to the same creator and their paths still end at the same place? They would be choosing to pray following their own path, their own faith, using their own religious and/or scientific terms to describe the same thing we are all seeking, to become one with our creator.

Isn't that what we all do when we pray; use a word that is personal to us? I had to find out what it was I believed. Who, what, was my God? Did I believe in science, religion, or both? Would I be able to incorporate both as one?

Religion taught me that God created the universe and filled it with light, a light which cannot exist without energy. From science I learned that all of creation resulted from a Big Bang filled with energy. Wouldn't it then be reasonable to merge the two as one field of energy?

This energy is everywhere; inside us and all around us, uniting everything on earth. It cannot be created nor can it be destroyed. Isn't that the way many of us think of the guiding force in the universe? I do, which is what made it easier for me to envision both the energy in the universe and God as *one* connecting us to all without any separation from what we feel but cannot see. I was finally able to understand that God is not apart from me, but an energy within me.

If spiritual relates to the human spirit or soul can we say God is a spiritual energy, one of love within, connecting us to all? Had I stumbled on something profound? Has it always been known from the beginning of time, or was this my time to understand that we are not separated from energy, not separated from anyone or anything in the universe, not separated from God or whatever word suits your personal belief. This seemed too simple. Maybe it is. Maybe that's intended.

Life, however, isn't simple. It's a complicated metamorphosis through which we balance our happiness and our grief.

"Your joy is your sorrow unmasked."
(Kahlil Gibran)

*"Death leaves a heartache no one can heal;
love leaves a memory no one can steal."*

From a headstone in Ireland

Chapter Four
The Unexplainable

Finally on the open road thinking that time was on my side, I drove leisurely down to Maryland where I was to meet my son and his family. The closer I got, the more urgently I felt that I was losing time. I arrived late afternoon, and we spent that first evening all together in one motel room. My daughter-in-law was very happy and looking forward to the beginning of a new life for all of them.

Sleep eluded all of us as we anticipated the events that would be taking place, and morning came early. It was moving day into their new home, and my two granddaughters, 4 years of age and 18 months, were eagerly looking forward to the excitement of the movers, exploring their new house, playing in their yard and meeting their new neighbors.

If only we were able to rewrite our life's script to alter the reality we were to face. Interrupting the joyful sounds of my granddaughters' laughter came the sound of three digits being dialed on the phone. My heart quickened. My son was dialing 911.

I walked around in a daze waiting to hear what was happening when I eventually saw my daughter-in-law walking slowly down the stairs. She was crying softly, holding the banister with one hand and covering her body with her other arm protecting her two unborn sons. I thought, *God, please, not the babies.*

Isn't that ironic. The first words uttered during a time of tragedy, whether or not one believes in God, are *God, please.* Our eyes met. Not a word had to be spoken. I could sense her saying to me, *make sure you take care of my girls,* as she walked to an ambulance waiting outside to transport her to the nearest hospital an hour or so away.

I went through the motions of unpacking boxes, one after the other, while my mind was obsessed with thoughts of and prayers for my daughter-in-law and the babies. Within three hours I received a call from my son. His words were brief. *Mom, we lost her.*

What was he saying, *we lost her?* That was impossible. She wasn't supposed to die. Where had things gone wrong? I couldn't believe that her life ended, making an about face towards death in as much time as it takes to attend a church service or see a movie. And what about the babies? Refusing to believe what I had heard, I feverishly continued unpacking the boxes in anticipation of my daughter-in-law and the twin boys returning home. That's what I wanted to believe. Instead I was taken to the hospital to say my last goodbye.

She was kept alive on life-support until her parents and family members flew down from Rhode Island to see her for the last time. How did this happen? Why did this happen? Without warning the life of this beautiful young woman was snuffed out in a matter of hours, catapulting everyone into a downward spiral … into heart-wrenching chaos. We were left grieving. We were left with a deep empty hole in our hearts, a hole that would remain within us forever.

Many hearts were wounded that fatal day when my daughter-in-law's life ended along with the lives of the five-month twin boys in utero. Time did not stand still for them. In three hours they were all gone. A close and loving family is a blessing, however, the deeper we love them, the more deeply we grieve, and the lonelier we are. We all flew back to her parents' home to make plans for the memorial service. With the love and support of family and friends who flew in to be with us, we somehow made it through the next couple of days.

***T**he evening of my daughter-in-law's memorial service, we were staying at her parents' home, trying to find the right words to say to our granddaughters who were confused, wondering where their mother was, why everyone was crying; trying to find the right words to say to each other that would help us all get through the night. We prayed exhaustion would overtake us, knowing that we would face life every day thereafter without her.*

By midnight there was a torrential storm. Flashes of lightening were booming like cannons. The crackling voltage was pounding against the windows, creating a staggering effect of a powerful force needing to gain entry. The rain that came with it seemed like gigantic tears crying to be with everyone inside. Did anyone hear what I did? Perhaps there was rain that night, thunder, and lightening, or it could have been a spiritual illumination of my daughter-in-law's cry to be inside with her family where she belonged.

My daughter-in-law's passing almost devastated my son completely. A horrible injustice had been done, and I was afraid I would also lose him. His aura had gone dark, almost non existent. An aura is an emanation that surrounds the body of every living creature. It's a magnetic energy in different colors that is sensed, felt, and even seen around a physical body. My son's aura was black and very thin, interrupting the three foot flow of energy around his body, indicating major depression and approaching death.

He had the responsibility of his daughters, and he had to somehow lift himself out of the depths of despair. I was helpless. Every minute of his life was marked by her absence, an absence present like a pain about which you have no control. Every action lacked substance because she was not there to share any of it with him.

The reality of her passing was all consuming. Without warning they were gone, an irrevocable finality. I wept for the conversations we would never have ... for the girls who would be without a mother ... for my son whose soul was shrinking into darkness. How was he going to let her go?

"I simply believe that some part of the human Self or Soul is not subject to the laws of space and time."

Carl Jung

Chapter Five
Discovering My Universe

"You don't have a soul. You are a soul."
(C.S. Lewis)

This feeling, this intuition, where does it originate? Is it the mind of God? Is God a universal intelligence? Everything we experience seems to have a ripple effect on everything else that follows. Beyond my comprehension, understanding did come to me in time.

One afternoon as I sat in my daughter's family room, my eyes focused on a wall hanging. As if in a trance-like state, I saw an image of the wall hanging begin to move. Keeping my focus on its center, the image moved to the right and remained there, as if signaling me to be prepared for what was about to happen.

It then slowly moved behind the center point to the left before returning back to its point of origin. It made a complete rotation, however, it did not stop there. The three images then moved parallel to each other, one superimposed over the other, and then returned back again to the center of the wall hanging. The movement had formed an image of itself in what seemed to be a holographic frame.

That experience enabled me to perceive of the possibility that all of space is throughout all of time. If this is so, that could mean the present, past, and future are all one, and we are living in a holographic universe of parallel dimensions separated only by the passing of time. And what is time but a creation by humans to make sense of reality. We are our own timekeeper.

This changed my thinking. Never having had a visual of God except as a spirit in the universe, and believing I am a physical extension of energy, when I now pray I reflect on the words collectively, from which and from whom all things come. However, I don't use them collectively. I continue to use the word that has always provided me a comfort zone, a word that has been part of my faith since childhood … God.

This does not negate your use of the term that means the most to you. I reference both God and energy, not to confuse or offend, but to enable you to better understand what I am trying to convey. If it is helpful, you may consider substituting the word

God with the word that means the most to you for clarity and better understanding.

Many people eventually wonder about the meaning of life, which never seems to reveal itself. Many also have suffered with restrictions, distortions, and the widespread opinion that their belief is wrong and struggle with those wanting to fit them within their own perspective.

We struggle with some questions; we grapple for some answers. The bottom line is there are no answers in this lifetime, and we look for like-minded people with whom to discuss our thoughts. I don't want to fit you into my belief, nor have I developed any new ideas. I'm simply writing what resulted from my experiences to help you understand how I came to this point in my life.

This concept continues to be difficult to explain in any way that I or anyone can truly understand, and attempts have often resulted in misconceptions. Some negate and/or refuse combining any type of scientific and/or religious explanation; some agree with one or the other; and some continue to remain on the fence until they reach a conclusion in their own time. I fall into the latter category, which conclusion wondrously changes over time.

At this moment it seems to me that if we are a physical extension of this energy, God, then the continuation of our soul with all our past knowledge is possible. Why not? Being an extension of spiritual energy means that nothing can be born of it or die of it. Being a part of this field of energy that permeates our huge universe means that this universe would be available to me simply because I believed in it.

That would be amazing! Merging both as one, perceiving it as a balance of yin and yang, one not existing without the other, would give me access to all things throughout time. If God, Eternity, exist outside of time, then every moment is the present, and it is in the present moment that we live.

Isn't that the phrase we often hear ... live in the moment? Just imagine if we could also see and be seen simultaneously throughout time in all our various stages - infancy, adolescence, young adulthood, middle aged, old - there would be no death as we know it.

This is profound. I want to believe there is no beginning and no end, then life could be perceived not only as a crossing over but also as a continuous thread blending lifetimes, blending centuries throughout space and time. I would no longer wonder where the past ends or the future begins. Everything and everyone would be right here with me. A heart within a heart in a place where there is no separation, a place where we are one ... one life, one love, one energy running through all.

What a magnificent thought. I want to be part of this marvelous existence. Although still an awkward concept, it made sense to me and began to influence me and the events in my life that followed. Everything happens for a reason.

"The past, present, and future are properties of consciousness."
(Author Unknown)

"Our souls traverse spaces in Life which are not measurable by Time, that invention of man."

Kahlil Gibran

Chapter Six
Time Travel

We go through life hearing of horrific tragedies. That they could someday happen to us is not in our consciousness. Not in mine. How would my son survive? If he couldn't let her go, his daughters would suffer. If he couldn't let her go, his wife would have hated it. I thought if they could be together in some way, she would be able to provide him with the strength to think of the lives of their daughters. It would be so easy if we were able to travel in time.

Why do we assume we can't, that we can only be at one place at one time? If we can understand that Eternity is never ending, then every point in the universe would be directly connected to every other point regardless of distance. Just think about it. If consciousness is both infinite and eternal, spreading across the universe everywhere all at once, it would be possible for us to have access to limitless dimensions and capabilities. It also would make it possible to have out-of-body experiences with our astral body, our mental body, which some call our intelligent soul.

Assuming this is possible, our souls would leave our present bodies and travel in time to various time periods with immeasurable speed. We would no longer be bound to the laws of gravity, time, and the physical world.

Moving about in time is a metaphysical activity rooted in the Greek word *me-ta-phy-si-ka*, which translates into after the things of nature. Out-of-body experiences or time travel may not yet be deemed normal behavior, however, they are possible - not just during the dying process. I accept it can happen because it happened to me.

I had just gone to bed. I longed for my children, not having seen them for weeks following my daughter-in-law's passing. I decided to meditate, hoping to receive some insight. I suddenly found myself out of my body and looking down at myself on the bed as I was moving about the room looking for a way out. I felt I would bang against the door and awoke with a start, not understanding what had happened. My heart was pounding. I understand some will question what I am about to say, however, if I knew then what I know now, I would have been able to go through the wall and connect with them, bringing each other the comfort we all needed.

A few years later I saw an old friend from high school and shared my experience. She told me that she often dreamed of reaching for something high and begin jumping, each jump bringing her higher to a place not necessarily her objective. There were times when her jumps would catapult her into flight above the water and the beach where she used to live, and she would be exhilarated by the experience, not fearful as I had been.

Once on the island of Nantucket, she discovered an old grist mill, similar to a stone tower, in which there was a large circular grist stone used to grind grain. She looked out of a small diamond-shaped window with grainy glass and not 100 yards away saw a group of approximately 50 horses galloping toward the building with men bare from the waist up. She screamed and crouched down covering her head.

Turning back a few moments later, there was no sight of them. Shaken, she told the guard at the mill what she had seen, and he told her that the window had been purposely built small to keep the native American Indians living nearby from entering. It only took a moment, but those men were as real to her as any people she had ever seen. With a veil between past, present, and future, who is to say that it did not happen.

One weekend I stayed with my two grandchildren who were toddlers at the time. I put both children in a bedroom next to mine to be able to respond to their awakenings or disturbances. A disturbance is what I encountered, but not theirs.

Awake in bed with the door open to hear the children if need be, I saw the shadow of a woman approaching my daughter's bedroom across the hall from my room. I began to panic. I didn't even have a phone in the room to call for help. Without thinking I jumped out of bed and intercepted an elderly woman at the doorway, staring into the room she had not yet entered. I asked her what she was doing breaking into the house. She looked at me and quietly said, 'I want to go home.'

I led her into the family room and sat down with her. She explained that she desperately needed to find her way back home. When asking her where she lived, she replied, 'the Ukraine.' I told her I would take her home. It's a huge mystery to me what happened next. I have no recollection of taking her there or how. My only memory is of her thanking me when we reached her door.

Having heard about life after death, I knew that some believe there are times when a soul is lost between the here and now. When my daughter and son-in-law returned home I told them what had occurred and asked if anyone had died in the house. My daughter acknowledged that indeed an older woman had died in the home they had recently purchased.

I asked my daughter if she knew where the woman came from. She didn't know for certain except that she was from Europe, possibly somewhere near Russia. It sounds unbelievable, doesn't it. How could it be verified and why would anyone question what was my reality?

"Who so loves, believes the impossible."

Elizabeth Barrett Browning

Chapter Seven
*S*urviving

This was the time before ultrasound when birth defects could not be detected in utero. There were so many babies in Intensive Care who were in far worse condition than my son. As bizarre as it may sound, I began to feel blessed that he *only* had a rare cardiac anomaly.

My son spent most of his first month of life at the hospital where loving staff tried to stabilize his tachycardia in preparation for the surgical procedure that would enlarge the hole between the three chambers of his heart. I learned with the touch of my fingers how fast his heart was racing, often counting up to an incredible number in the high 300s.

I travelled into the city every day, staying with my son from early morning until late at night, returning home where my mother was providing loving care for my first-born son. During that time I had many opportunities to hold my baby in my arms. As young as he was, he would lift his head up straight, stretch his neck back, and stare at me with his eyes wide open as if questioning me. He was no longer smiling, and I struggled with what he was thinking.

I was his mother, the one who was to protect him from harm. I was in torment. As parents we focus on what we need to do to protect our children. How could I? I felt guilty. All I could think of was that he was questioning why I was allowing this to happen to him. I cried for all that he was going through. I couldn't bear the sight of those difficult painful procedures being inflicted upon my little baby.

I couldn't endure that pain, how could *he,* being prodded with needles and syringes in his tiny arms, on his legs, upon his ankles, and in his head? He was my child and to this day the painful memory continues to haunt me.

I was in agony. I was bewildered not understanding why or how it happened, berating myself that it may have been or was my fault. I had been teaching throughout my pregnancy, and some of my students had German Measles, which is known can affect the development of the heart in utero. Was it me? Could I have passed on this anomaly? Did we possibly have cardiac anomalies in our DNA? Or was it meant to happen?

My son was in and out of the hospital many times the first few years of his life, and for many years thereafter. My mother continued to care for my first born son and later my new-born baby daughter. What a burden I placed upon her ... one she accepted without question, administering support and love to my children, putting my mind at ease.

My children needed me, and I wouldn't be with them. As a mother how could I choose? How would I choose? The answer always was to be with the one in most need. Right or wrong, we do what we need to do at the moment, and I chose to be with the one struggling to live. That didn't stop me from feeling guilty that I was failing my other children who also needed me.

I was terrified of what could happen. Should I formulate a plan? How could I? I didn't even know what quality of life my son would have or how much he would be able to do. What I did know, however, was that I was going to do all that was in my power to make it as normal and enjoyable as possible.

He had so much love from everyone, everywhere, praying for his well being, and in time he became a happy baby again. We would laugh lovingly at his funny antics, and he would look up at us and smile a contagious smile that filled me, filled all of us with warmth and love.

One would never know that he was compromised. We learned to look for those times when his lips and nails would become dark from lack of oxygen. I prayed that he would always know how much I loved him ... that if I had the power to have changed the circumstances of his birth, I would have absorbed it all myself. But I couldn't. *Why did it have to be my baby? Why couldn't it have been me?*

How far back does memory go?

How much would my son remember of his early childhood? Do children remember what they did, what they endured? Do they remember their life before birth? Do we? How much are we able to retain until the veil of separation emerges and memory of previous lifetimes shuts down?

I believe children do remember, and they can see. You must surely have heard of youngsters talking with imaginary friends. Are they all imaginary, or is that the easiest way to explain that phenomenon?

***S**he was a youngster at the time when she first began talking about someone visiting her. She finally described him to her parents, and her mother knew immediately that it was an uncle who had passed away years before her granddaughter's birth. No one knew why he chose to come to her … except perhaps as a child she was still receptive to experiences that crossed the time barrier, and he had a message to share.*

If we believe there is a continuation of life, it is conceivable to say we *are* born with knowledge in its entirety, carrying it with us before birth throughout each eternal stage, and the things that happen to us before we are born affect us.

We move through life each and every day in a manner that would never have been there if it weren't for our ancestors. We are profoundly connected to them, to generations yet to come, and to those who have come before us. Is the fate of each the fate of all?

Have you ever wondered if we have the power before birth to choose our parents, the ones who will help us with the lessons we are to learn in this lifetime?

If we choose to accept that we are born with the knowledge of all, then I believe we *do* have the power to choose our parents. How special it was that my son chose me as his mother! How blessed I am that in his learning, he taught me.

Gregory of Nyssa, venerated as a saint in many religions such as Roman Catholicism, Eastern Orthodoxy, Oriental Orthodoxy, Anglicanism, preached that the soul is on an infinite journey towards God, never reaching but always drawing closer and becoming more intimate.

In our present lifetime our body is temporary, and our soul goes on forever surviving throughout Eternity.

"All I have seen teaches me to trust the Creator for all I have not seen."

Ralph Waldo Emerson

Chapter Eight
Forever Present

Have you ever been with a dying person when life ends? I have, a number of times. When they close their eyes in death of their present being, their final breath is exhaled. I see the movement of their chest and feel I can actually see the exhale, like a soundless *poof.* My feeling is that they begin to live with a new set of eyes, similar to when we close our eyes in meditation, lift the veil separating time, and begin to see the place where earth and sky are one, making life a continual renewal.

I agree that this is difficult to understand, however, if we are created with this consciousness, it would seem we would be able to communicate with individuals who have crossed over. More often than not, but not always, communication occurs in times of crises or need. Although loved ones who have crossed over may be moving toward oneness in the universe, evolving over many lifetimes, they are always near us. There is never a moment when they do not come to us in some form or another, whether we seek them or not.

Butterflies are the sign of renewal. They symbolize rebirth. If we compare the similarity of souls leaving their bodies as they're crossing over to those of caterpillars leaving their cocoons, then once dead they experience a serenity and beauty which they bring to the people around them.

Butterflies often surrounded my granddaughter, beginning the day of her mother's memorial service. Who is to say that was not a sign of her mother watching over her, bringing her a quiet calm and peace?

***M**y granddaughter was only four when her mother died. Just three months after her mother's death, she was a flower girl at my daughter's wedding. It was strange to her that life was going on without her mother. She was frightened, still trying to make sense of how and why her mother was no longer alive. Hesitant to walk down the aisle toward the altar by herself, her father told her to stay very focused and to look at him - that he would be waiting for her at the front of the church. And she did just that.*

Holding the flowers in her hand and containing her tears, she walked directly down the aisle. Staring straight ahead, it appeared as if she was slowly being pulled by an imaginary thread connecting her to the front of the church, almost as if she was in a trance looking at what was before her.

At the end of the ceremony I asked her if she was looking at her father, who as best man was standing on the right side of the altar. She answered that she was indeed looking at him, and then added that she was also looking at her mother, who was standing on the left side of the altar, encouraging her to walk towards them both.

On a number of occasions as we were about to have dinner and I was to take my seat at the table, my granddaughter would stop me saying, 'Yiayia, be careful. You can't sit there. Mom is sitting there tonight.' She never asked me if I was able to see her mother. She must have taken it for granted that I did. Why wouldn't I? And I never questioned her; I believed her. Those we love who have crossed over are always with us.

Having left one life do we leave our loved ones behind? Can we come back? There are times when I feel my daughter-in-law has moved on, but not in any usual manner of reincarnation. I have learned that it often takes many years of introspection for the soul to decide on reincarnation, also called rebirth, and what is to be carried into the new life, into the new body. Rebirth is shared by many religions, and in Ancient Greece it found a place in the philosophical teachings of Plato.

I had a dream that my daughter-in-law tried to convince the elders on the astral plane, a higher spiritual realm of existence, to allow her to reincarnate almost immediately. My understanding is that it takes at least 20 years or more before reincarnation can occur; perhaps as many as 60 years, which in many cultures is the recurring timespan. I envisioned an alternative.

My daughter-in-law and daughter were the best of friends. Since my granddaughter had said that her mother was standing by the front pew at my daughter's wedding, it could have been possible that my daughter-in-law had found a way to connect with her. Within a few months after the wedding I learned that my daughter had conceived in Greece on her honeymoon. One of my daughter-in-law's happiest memories was her trip there with my son. Although a stretch of my imagination, I considered this information meaningful and connected my imaginary lines.

I often have dreams that repeat themselves and continue at a later time. This was one of them. My dream did not include the gender of the baby, only that the baby's name would begin with the letter 'L.' My son had an endearing nickname for my daughter-in-law which began with the letter 'L.' My daughter gave birth, and unaware of my dream, gave her son a name beginning with the letter 'L.' Coincidentally, my daughter-in-law's sister gave birth the same month. Two babies died July 2000, and two babies within the same family circle were born July 2001.

I don't believe my daughter-in-law reincarnated, but I do believe it's possible that the love she had for her sister and sister-in-law crossed time and space in a significant way and became a living memory. I know it sounds ludicrous, but I liken it to the recipient of an organ transplant who has a miraculously strong connection with an unknown organ donor that cannot logically be explained. We have no way of knowing, however, miracles do come to us in unusual ways.

"The golden moments in the stream of life rush past, and we see nothing but sand; the angels come to visit us, and we only know them when they're gone."

George Elliot

Chapter Nine
Angels On Earth

Mothers are meant to comfort their children. I could not console my son to lessen his grief. I could not bring back the mother and twin brothers my four-year-old and eighteen month-old granddaughters were expecting to return.

Five weeks had passed since their tragic deaths. So much pain; so many tears. Five weeks trying to hold together the lives of my son and granddaughters whose hearts were pierced by the death of wife and mother. Five long weeks living with her parents who had lost forever one of their irreplaceable joys. Five weeks trying to keep my soul from splitting apart.

I felt helpless in easing anyone's grief. I was desperate to get away by myself before I shattered. My sister offered me the use of her condo on a lake in upstate New York, and I began my eleven hour journey with no perception of distance or where I was heading. I only knew I had to go.

I had forgotten how beautiful that area is … the lakes and hills, almost like a bit of yesteryear when the simplicities of life brought people together … happy times, which for me was a life that was no longer possible. The beauty surrounding me didn't help. The beautiful woman I loved was gone, and I really didn't care about anything else.

Alone with my thoughts and no one to hear me, I started shouting loudly in anguish, hoping somehow my life would return to normal. Driving became the catalyst which enabled me to sob unconsolably. Eight hours into the trip, my grief exploded a torrential downpour, and the floodgates of my soul opened. Five weeks of pent-up emotion cascaded down my face. It was desolate at that time in the early evening; no glaring headlights; nothing to distract me. I had an open road to let my life take its own course, and I didn't care where that would be … anywhere away from this incurable pain in my heart.

My sobbing became uncontrollable, and then something extraordinary happened. A white bird abruptly swept down in front of my windshield, startling me, causing me to veer towards the shoulder of the road. For a brief moment I feared I would crash. Crashing was something I could handle; my daughter-in-law's death was not. I kept wiping my glasses with my hands as my tears continued, and my car was driving itself nearing 100 miles an hour.

Just as suddenly, there it was again; this time with much more force. A white bird flew back and forth across my windshield three times, close enough for me to flinch. How dare that bird try to interfere in changing my course. I wanted to forget all that had happened. I wanted everything to return to normal. I wanted my daughter-in-law and the twin boys back. That damn bird! Where did it come from? And then as suddenly as it had appeared, it was gone again. Where had it gone? How did it disappear so quickly from my line of vision? Was it only one bird or was it three birds? How could it appear and disappear with such intensity? Was I hallucinating?

It was then I realized it had been flying specifically for me. During this time when I was in my worst frame of mind, an angel had appeared in the form of a white bird, warning me to slow down, to take control of myself, my car, my life. This was a sign I could not refute.

As my tears subsided, three white birds in formation flew in front of my windshield bringing me back to my present reality. I took a deep breath and was immediately filled with an overwhelming calm. The three white birds, my white angels, once more swept in front of my windshield as if saying, you'll be okay now, bidding me goodbye.

Were the angels watching over me my daughter-in-law and the twin boys, or my son, my brother, and my brother-in-law who had crossed over much too early in life? Either of these answers could be valid, but irrelevant. The relevance is in the knowledge and belief that there is no death, that our loved ones are always with us and often send us signs. Sometimes it takes a little miracle to remind us that we are never alone and always in the presence of angels.

Angels are not figments of wishful thinking; they are real. Would it be easier for you if you were to conceive of them as being people of exemplary compassion, love, and virtue, and not limit yourself trying to understand them as messengers with wings and feathers? It seems to me we can see them in a way we can understand, in a way that makes sense to us at the time. They are here all around us in some form – seen and unseen.

Your understanding or acceptance of this phenomenon is left entirely to your individual belief. If it is true, however, that we can connect with angels at the time of crossing over, then, more significantly, it would follow that we could interact with them during other phases of our life, which is exactly what happened to me.

I don't claim to understand everything or anything, but what would we lose if we learn to open our third eye to the possibility of understanding that which we feel is not yet understandable?

Life is amazing … somewhere between extraordinary and majestic.

"… don't believe what your eyes are telling you. All they show is imitation. Look with your understanding, find out what you already know and you'll see the way to fly."
(Jonathan Livingston Seagull)

*"...I believe in everything
until it's disproved...
It all exists, even if it's in your mind."*

John Lennon

Chapter Ten
Understanding My Reality

I was fortunate to be able to walk to the public library by going out the rear gate of the condominium complex in which I lived. It was 2004. One day I noticed an announcement of an upcoming speaker, Brian Greene. I had never heard of him, however, he was going to speak on time and space, referring to his two books, *The Elegant Universe* and *The Fabric of the*

Cosmos, both of which interested me. They reminded me of a book I had read years before by Alan Lightman. Lightman's *Einstein's Dreams* was a collage of 30 short stories involving a conception of time. This was my opportunity I thought to help me understand time-space reality, although sitting through a scientific lecture would most likely be incomprehensible to me, especially one on Quantum Physics.

I was in for a surprise. Brian Greene, theoretical physicist and Professor of Physics at Columbia University, is a fabulous lecturer. In simple terms he gave me a very basic introduction to Quantum Physics and the String Theory. I actually understood what it is and what it could mean to me.

I was a child of the radio generation, and it made sense to me when he spoke of hundreds of different radio waves, minuscule strands of energy, each being broadcast with its own frequency and energy. I learned that each one of us is tuned in to one of these frequencies ... the one that corresponds to our vibration. Once leaving the lecture, I felt that in which I believed was a possibility - that heaven *is* here on earth, and we *can* be connected to all.

Soon thereafter I was introduced to the concept of quantum healing. Difficult as it was to understand, I learned that our DNA is a complete blueprint of every cell in our body, *that every cell has intelligent knowledge of thoughts, feelings, and body conditions through a constant stream of information.* Although challenging for me to fully understand, in a strange way it also made some sense to me. I so wanted to believe that the body, mind, and soul are connected and in communication.

As a first generation American of Hellenic heritage, English was not my first language. I wanted to share my thoughts with someone who would put skepticism aside and try to understand what seemed unrealistic and impossible for me to understand. Sadly I kept the thoughts to myself, but in time a concept was revealed to me that I could understand.

The way I now look at it, living life, interpreting reality, is an art with no rules. Our life is our canvas. We are the artist, which is the basis for my choosing the opening quote of this book by celebrated Greek writer, poet, and philosopher, Nikos Kazantzakis. If our reality depends upon what we are willing to imagine and allow, then anything that can be perceived must be reality, our reality.

Deepak Chopra, MD., an advocate of alternative healing who preaches the mind-body connection, suggests that this knowledge is liberating, a vision similar to that of George Berkeley, Irish priest and philosopher. We have the freedom to dance to our own tune, beat to our own drum, and I believe that someone who has the ability to translate that vibration will perceive it. How're you doing with mine?

Thanks to Brian Greene I was now receptive to the idea that my frequency was going to help me understand what I was feeling and capable of seeing and understanding. Each of us is a single cell, and cells in the universe are all the same, working in clusters of little machines within a bigger machine. How they vibrate and interact make them unique and connect us to this bigger machine.

I refer to the bigger machine as the power of One - God's spiritual energy as the One that eternally keeps our souls connected exactly as they are in the present, past, and future. It is always there. We don't have to seek it. We just need to feel it.

How much do we know? There are times I think I don't know anything at all, paraphrasing Socrates, a classical Greek philosopher, especially between human knowledge and the realm of spiritual energy and God in the universe. I'm always searching, however, at this moment in time I believe that every aspect of our earthly life is recorded from day one, but for reasons unknown our previous lives are blocked from our consciousness.

That doesn't mean they don't exist. That doesn't mean they can't be accessed. I accessed two of my past lives with the help of a meditation mediator who guided me through a regression process. First priming my unconscious with a series of questions, the mediator's goal was for me to gain direct knowledge and experience about myself as a soul journeying and growing through time towards healing and oneness.

I wanted to learn what I had done in my past lives and how they may have impacted me in my present life. The first time I participated I learned that I was a teacher in an orphanage; in the second, I was an orphan. I believed it because what I discovered about myself validated what I was doing in this life, perhaps even why and how I was choosing to do so. I was happy with those visions.

I learned that my life's purpose is one of giving and receiving through teaching … all ages, all levels, various topics … with a positive spirt and love that makes learning a fun and exciting experience, one which joyously continues to drive every aspect of my professional and personal life.

*"My mother...is my blood...
the beating of my heart.
I cannot now imagine a life without her."*

Kristin Hannah

Chapter Eleven
Learning From My Parents

If we believe we choose our parents, which I do, I could not have chosen a better couple to have helped me learn the lessons I needed to learn in this lifetime. They taught me not by telling me what to do, but by showing me in the manner they each lived their lives. They both offered me the best they had to give; each one different.

Parents ... both became a blending of role models for me.

My father taught me to be carefree, to live in the moment, sing, play cards, be social, not feel intimated to laugh out loud, be a risk taker against all odds, and to believe there are individuals who can communicate with those who have crossed over. All of which he did and passed on to me. The relationship between my father and me was unique.

My mother taught me determination, humility, honesty, endurance, kindness, to think with compassion, and to believe we can communicate through dreams with those who have crossed over. All of which she did and passed on to me. Although the relationship between my mother and me was not always an easy one, she is the one who impacted me the most.

The divide between my mother and me may be called unconscious rejection. She came to a new and strange country as a young bride, not knowing the language. She immediately became pregnant with my brother and again with me two months after his birth.

Perhaps throughout our lives she was unconsciously trying to overcome the initial guilt of rejecting me upon conception and was never able to overcome her inability to physically express her love for me. If I had been an orphan in a previous life, as I had learned during a past life regression, could possibly explain my need for greater affection throughout my life.

There were precious moments lost between us, however, in time I changed. I came to the realization that she loved me in her own quiet way, and whatever occurred or didn't occur was the way she was able to cope with her life, and coping was a lesson that served me very well later in life. I began to recall and appreciate all the wonderful things she had done for me, and I was flooded with memories of how much she supported me, how much she taught me, instead of what she was unable to express.

Mama was noble, thoughtful, and never spoke in a negative manner against anyone, even if they had wounded her deeply. I was amazed at what she accomplished … marrying at the age of 14 in a rural village in Greece, coming to America, and in the process of growing up and growing old, she taught herself to read, write, and speak English.

Breakfasts with my mother were special and full of surprise. Mama had a unique gift of connecting with people who had passed or were about to pass. Dreams shared by Mama were not a figment of her imagination. In the morning over coffee she would share her dreams … who she saw, what they said, what they did, what it was like.

Mama had been raised in a religious way with a grandfather who was a priest, both loving and domineering in the old school. At first I never fully knew if she believed in her dreams, however, her expression said it all, and I believed everything she told me as she saw it.

One morning she told me of seeing my children's father who had been hospitalized for many months. Both Mama and I shared the same vision that night, that when she died, he would follow her within a short period of time. And he did - one month to the date of Mama's death.

Communicating with the deceased were not figments of my parents' imagination. Don't look for any authentication. There is none. It was the truth as they saw it. I believed it. I believed them, without any earthly verification, and I began to have my own experiences.

For several years Mama had dreams of my son and my father dressed in white, as if in preparation for her visit. They in fact had died many years before her. To be able to see, communicate with and feel the presence of those who have crossed over or will cross would be proof that there is no time or space except in our minds. It's very hard to imagine that we could very well be living in Eternity.

Although I knew Mama was coming to the end of her life, I did not believe she would give up when she did. We had flown from Florida to Georgia to be with my daughters for Thanksgiving when she fell into distress. She was admitted to the Emergency Room and diagnosed with severe dehydration. Numerous attempts to insert an IV line into her proved futile. Mama winced, but never uttered a sound. It was when they were trying in her head, that Mama said, *'Stamata.'* Stop. No more. It was painful to watch.

When asked by the staff what she had said and what they should do, my sister and I looked at each other, neither one of us wanting to make a decision. However, neither one of us wanted her to continue suffering; most of all neither did Mama, and I as the oldest said, *'Stop. No more,'* feeling I was ending Mama's life.

I felt a deja-vu back to the time when I had to say similar words with regard to my son. But my son did survive and maybe Mama would. She was discharged, and my sister and I stayed with her at a motel near the hospital waiting and hoping she would regain her strength and we would take her back home to Florida.

At the end of the first week my eldest son was to be ordained a priest in Wisconsin, and I went to be with him promising to return immediately. Mama may have secretly been hoping my son would return with me. All her grandchildren were special, equal among equals, each with their individual charisma, but he was her first grandchild. He was special to her; he had suffered grief that was impossible for her to bear. She never did get over it.

It is known in many cultures that people who are approaching death *will* themselves to wait until the loved ones they are waiting for come to see them. Mama could have been waiting for my son, or just waiting for me. When I returned, I shared with her the details of my son's ordination, and two days later she succumbed.

Failure to survive is what they called it. Grief is what I called it. Her body was failing because she was no longer able or willing to cope with the death of those who were young, my daughter-in-law's death specifically because she never had a chance to say goodbye.

We're not supposed to outlive our children and grandchildren; outliving them both was too difficult for her. It is said that depression causes forgetfulness, however, for Mama, her depression was because she couldn't forget, and she just gave up. She crossed over with her daughters by her side soon after some of her grandchildren and great grandchildren visiting her had left. We should all be that fortunate. We should all be that blessed.

In the 6th century BC pre-Socratic Greek philosopher Parmenides said, *Existence is timeless*, a theory which influenced Western philosophy.

I want to believe there is no separation of time - that there is no here and there, just fluid movement. That could mean that heaven is not elsewhere, and we're never truly separate from those we love. Does being here with us mean we can communicate with them?

*"Accept the things to which fate binds you,
and love the people with whom fate
brings you together,
but do so with all your heart."*

Marcus Aurelius

Chapter Twelve
Communicating Across Boundaries

As human beings we are intricately interconnected with those who have died, as well as with all those in the generations yet to come. Choosing to believe there is no death and that life continues without the constraints of time, makes it possible to believe that we can easily connect with those who are yet to come and most importantly with those who have already crossed over.

More and more people are experiencing those phenomena and talking about them, making them known to those still filled with doubt - not to change their minds, but to help them consider what may be possible.

Communicating across boundaries, seen and unseen, happens in different forms … through prayer, angels, time travel, direct communication. It's not always something we've requested, often coming unrequested when the time is right. I'm not certain we all hear or want to hear what is being said.

Although we are able to have a mystical experience when we are not ready, I believe it gets logged until the proper time and place. It does seem to me, however, that the best experiences come to us when we are ready for them, and that's when we can choose to consider the possibility that they could be true.

There were a number of occasions when I felt the air move as if someone had entered my home. The first time it happened I immediately went into my bedroom and shut the door. Laying there not moving, I suddenly felt a weight on the bed, as if someone was gently sitting on the edge. It was then that a warm feeling engulfed me.

I could not see my son but I sensed him near me, and reaching out I felt the indentation on the bed. Have you ever felt that? I so missed his presence. He told me he was more than okay, and for me to stop worrying - that when loved ones worry it oftentimes keeps the soul from continuing on. I never kept him from doing anything when he was alive, I certainly wasn't going to do it now.

From that day forward I tried to live with a renewed faith, trying not to be fretful about how he was, although there are still moments when I question the validity of my feelings. I'd like to think the change in me resulted from a sense of calmness that came over me that night, somehow giving me the strength and courage to go on. It does for many, and it did for me.

During the last couple of months of his life, my father was living with my sister. I missed seeing him, and whenever I would call to speak with him, he was either asleep or unavailable. When he died quite quickly, I was devastated. I had wanted to see him, just one last time, to hug him and tell him how much I loved him.

A few months after his death, I felt the air move in the darkness of my bedroom, and I heard the soft sound of his voice telling me he has always known how much I loved him. You can choose to say that I imagined his voice because I wanted to hear it, or you can choose to say it really did happen because it could be possible.

The air is full of molecules and holds many secrets, producing aromas in certain combinations that can bring us back to a point of remembrance. There are times when certain sounds and visuals enable me to sense them. We all have our own individual scents, and this primal sense of smell always let me know when they were around. Is this scent, this essence, part of the soul?

It must be that unseen spiritual connections unify life. How else can we sense the air move, hear voices, and feel the presence of those we love? Life is mysterious and unpredictable.

My father had been a very heavy smoker from the age of nine when he rolled his own cigarettes in the field of the village in which he grew up. There are times, wherever I am and I smell smoke as if coming from a lit cigarette, I look around, and with no apparent reason or evidence of anyone smoking, I feel the essence of my father and know he is with me.

I do not smoke. I do not like the smell of smoke. On those occasions, however, I have the strongest desire to light up a cigarette and join him. No words. Just the wonderful feeling of being with him. On many of my trips to Greece when I am in the mountain region of his village, I roll a cigarette and think of him. The smell of smoke will always remind me of my father, and I embrace it, keeping that special moment in time a part of my memory.

Connection comes to us at different times in different forms and oftentimes humor is not lost.

Her mother had suffered a stroke and was in a coma. She knew that a person in a coma is able to hear what is going on around them, and she sat by her mother's bedside continuously talking to her. After five days, her mother opened her eyes, looked at her daughter, and in no uncertain terms said, 'Did you have to talk incessantly; you were non-stop.'

She also shared with her daughter her experience while in the coma. She saw a bright light and felt she was being beckoned to walk toward it. 'Oh, no,' her mother said, 'I'm not ready to go down that road. I still have a lot of living to do.'

When his mother was in and out of consciousness for a couple of months, I suggested he pay special attention to what she was saying, and not to dismiss what may seem to be impossible. She told him about having ice cream with her mother. 'Mom,' he said, 'you do know Yiayia is dead.' 'Of course,' she responded, 'but she's with me now, and we're eating ice cream together.'

Prior to his death he told his wife that when he died she would know whenever he was around because he would come to her as a grasshopper. They both laughed at the thought. She did laugh, with tears, when one day shortly after he died, desiring his comfort, there appeared a grasshopper next to her … in an apartment they shared on the tenth floor of their New York City apartment building.

I used to teach Greek to a woman who worked at Pratt & Whitney. She had previously told me that her brother was killed on September 11th by the plane that crashed into the Twin Towers. She knew from previous conversations that I believed in an afterlife, and one day she asked me whether I believed communicating with the dead was possible.

I told her all I knew, what I had read and experienced, that oftentimes the repetition of a prayer and its vibration enables those who have crossed over to come to them. It is also possible for that phenomenon to occur in reverse, in that those who have crossed over need to communicate with those who are still living, and their vibrations match.

She needed to communicate with her brother and prayed that he would come to her because there were problems brewing within the family that involved his young daughter, *born shortly after September 11th, and the child's grandmother, their mother.*

One day prior to class she told me her brother had come to her at night a number of times since our conversation months before, and they had discussed the family problem. During a visit she asked him to tell her of that horrific day on September 11th when lives ended so tragically. He told her that he did not recall suffering at all and assured her that upon death there is no pain. However, it was unbearable for him to recall the images of the faces of the suffering souls who had not yet died and asked that she never mention it again.

After another few months had passed, he came to her to tell her he was no longer going to communicate with her. Although the family issue had not yet been resolved, he felt it was heading in a positive direction, and from that day forward he would be communicating directly with his little daughter instead. As far as I know that indeed was what happened.

Life is mysterious and unpredictable.

> *"Youth ... the promise of happiness;
> life ... the realities of grief."*
>
> *Nicholas Sparks*

Chapter Thirteen
The **Promise** *Of* **Youth**

I did not treat my son as if he had a serious cardiac anomaly. I was not going to limit him or suffocate him by choosing his activities. I learned the love that doesn't say no because of my personal fears and allowed him to be like any other child - ride his bike, run, play ball, do whatever he wanted, whatever he was capable of doing. This was his life, and he had to live it his way.

And he did. He found ways that gave him a sense of belonging, like playing percussion in the school band, and despite the fact that he was limited in his physical activities, becoming manager of the basketball team made him feel he was an important member of his peer group's activities.

What he gave that was his alone to give was his beautiful artistic talent, and his work hangs in our homes today. Had I not given him the freedom to choose what he wanted to do, I would have cheated him of the greatest accomplishment of his life. As much as we want to protect our children, and I so wanted to protect him, the lessons of life are theirs to learn, and I firmly believe that's what enabled him to be a happy creative child, bringing joy into the lives of all the people he touched.

Although we realized the seriousness of his cardiac condition, we rarely talked about it. He never complained and lived without self-pity and melodrama. It was ever-present in our lives, and I tried not to show any outward worry about him; his siblings not imagining or wanting to imagine his condition to be as serious as it was.

Throughout his life he was in and out of the Emergency Room so often that it began to seem like a routine. The caring staff became his friends, and his hospital admissions became a normal part of his life that he would always endure, and where he felt safe and loved.

My son had so many arrhythmia that I stopped thinking about him as being sick. I didn't think of these Emergency Room visits as being dangerous near-death visits. He would be under control in a few hours and would be heading home to what was normal for us - each time terrified that he wouldn't be able to breathe again and his heart would stop forever. It killed me slowly, little by little, filling me with incredible fear that we would lose him. But we didn't, and each time my faith became stronger and helped me survive, and denial was dismissed.

Those years were not without tears or close calls. My son went through more surgical procedures and hospital admissions than most people would have in ten lifetimes. The other children in the hospitals were in far graver danger than he, far more limited. Parents huddled together crying at their inability to change the circumstances and help their children. God was watching out for my son, and I never stopped praying, overwhelmed with feeling truly blessed. This child was our greatest gift, bringing the entire family immeasurable happiness.

When he was 15 years old without warning his heart suddenly went into fibrillation lasting for many months. Fibrillation is the rapid, irregular, and unsynchronized contraction of the heart, fatal if not reversed by defibrillation and is usually a common cause of cardiac arrest.

For unexplainable reasons defibrillation did not work. That was another beginning - this time leading to an eventual end, never knowing which day would be his last, and still hoping it would never come.

This did not change his outlook on life. What did change radically was his appearance. As the layers of fat began to vanish, he began to look like a skeleton disguised with skin and protruding stomach. He was so beautiful to me. I looked beyond his physical appearance and saw the boy I loved, as beautiful as ever. Being with him I always felt as if my heart was warm and filled with love unending.

As his body was becoming thinner neither my mother nor I could look at the emaciated children of Africa on television without seeing him. I was told by his doctors that no matter how much he ate, his organism would digest its protein, the muscle would disappear, and his body would not have any power of resistance left. Why did they feel they needed to give me this descriptive explanation? I didn't want any.

He would look in the mirror, and say, *'Look at what I've become,'* and I would say, *'I see the same loving, happy beautiful child I've always known. It's what's inside that counts, not what you look like on the outside.'* I hoped he understood what I was saying, that he was deeply loved and always would be. To this day I continue to use the phrase, *It's what's inside that counts,* hoping everyone could learn to feel incredible joy emanating from within.

Remembering my son's long difficult journey and ongoing confrontations consumed me. I was facing the darkest days of my life, and something soundless in the depths of my soul was crying out. I was numb. I couldn't breathe. I felt the air was being sucked out of me. My beautiful son was going to die, and I would still be alive. It isn't supposed to be that we parents outlive our children.

There's something earthshaking about the unconditional love we have for our children. My heart was breaking little by little, piece by piece. I had four other children whom I loved very much. Being their parent was a daunting responsibility. Would I have anything left to give to them? Would home ever be the same again?

There were times I felt a grave sadness being a mother - unable to intercede in protecting my children from the harmful elements and tragedies in life. I gave birth to five children. It was calming to know they would always have each other if something happened to me. That equation was about to change.

One night late October my son was admitted to the hospital in New Haven. The doctors said his time was limited. What did that mean? His time couldn't be limited. He always pulled through, and he would again. His body had ceased to respond and was slowly breaking down. By midnight his kidneys had failed. The doctors tried every medication and intervention known to them, and nothing worked.

Shortly after 1 am he said, 'Enough, Mom, no more.' His time had come. The doctors looked at me and asked what they should do. The most difficult words I had to say, knowing I would be saying them for the last time, were 'no more.' That's what my son wanted, and he fell into a coma. There was no hope for him, but I never stopped praying, talking to him, telling him I was not ready to let him go. I prayed to God pleading for help. My son was ready to go, but I still wasn't ready to let him go; I didn't know if I ever would be.

As I prayed by his bedside what I didn't do was call his father, who had been there earlier in the evening, asking him to return. Because of this I felt I was somehow impeding my son's survival and felt unworthy of being granted the miracle of his life. I realized that subconsciously I was harboring anger with his father for failing in his responsibility to care for him.

But who was I to punish him by keeping him from his son? I never kept him from his son before, why now? He had every right to be there. The only way I would ever find peace was to let the past be the past, and I knew what I had to do. I called his father and told him to come to the hospital because we were losing our son.

In the early morning hours, the Intensive Care Unit was filled with family members. My son suddenly opened his eyes, looked at everyone in the room, and jumped out of bed. He told them how happy he was to see them, as he walked around the room being his usual gregarious self as if nothing had happened the night before. He loved family gatherings and told us he was looking forward to celebrating Thanksgiving and Christmas.

I had been aware that people who are on the verge of death have what is called a 'surge' where they appear to become well. The surge would last as long as the dying felt necessary, the length of time differing for every individual. Maybe his surge was because he knew I still wasn't ready to let him go, and once again he was Graced by God.

My mind spiraled back fifteen years in time when my smiling Irishman was five days old and not expected to live the night, and he was Graced. The love I have for my son sticks in the chambers of my heart. How could I live those years over again and remake our lives? I couldn't. It remains a remembering. It remains a painful longing.

I believe this time it was not only prayer, but my release of the anger I was harboring on a subconscious level. Once in a while our life changes for the better in one single moment. My forgiveness and love enabled my son to be Graced once again and also healed me. I felt unworthy to have been included in that moment, but I was, and I don't know why. Having been blessed, however, I know that God was with me and somehow I know He always will be.

During his time with me, when his life was ebbing, my son began to journey beyond this life to the next. What he saw and learned is the knowledge he left with me. His courage gave me the ability to see. He was and to this day remains my beacon of hope.

"I dream of things that never were, and ask why not?"

Robert Kennedy

Chapter Fourteen
Dreams **O**r **F**antasy

The study of dreams, oneirology, from the Greek word o-nei-ro, has long been a topic of discussion. Considered the universal language of the mind, dreams are sequences of images and/or sensations that occur during certain stages of sleep, revealing aspects of life from the past, present, and future.

Dreams shared by Mama were not a figment of her imagination ... nor mine. I believed her, and I had my own. I dream often and awaken before reaching an ending, which is not unusual. What is unusual is when I go back to sleep, I pick up the dream exactly where I left off; sometimes as many as four times in succession in the same evening. Upon awakening I may receive a thought I had never considered to a problem I was having, or reach a resolution to an issue with which I was struggling, or just a remembrance of an interesting dream. I shared this with a friend of mine, and this is what she shared with me.

Her grandmother was to undergo surgery. The night before her admission, she had a dream in which an angel came to her and told her she was not to have the operation, that it was no longer necessary. It awakened her, and she was distraught. Eventually falling back to sleep, the angel returned, advising her to spend the evening in prayer seeking good health.

She was a pious woman her entire life, one who also had the ability to see situations that would come true in the future. She did as she was told - to pray for good health, although that's what she would have done without the dream. The next morning during her pre op examination, the doctor was stunned. There was no trace of any health issue. Although not knowing why, he didn't discount the strength of prayer and what she had dreamed.

Although she had been visiting the hospital every day, on that day she didn't arrive in time to see her mother before she died. One night as she was praying for solace, she felt the nearness of her. Upon awakening she saw a vivid image of her mother with her beautiful silver hair. Her mother had a big smile *on her face, and appeared happy. What she saw was so real, as if she was there with her.*

They looked directly into each others' eyes, and although there were no words spoken, her mother's eyes said it all. Believing that the eyes are the window to the soul, she felt this was her mother's way of saying goodbye to her. She didn't need any validation of what she had seen. She believed it, and she accepted it. It brought her solace; it brought her closure.

***H**e had a dream about his cousin with whom he shared a close relationship and was anxious to share it with her. When she answered the phone, he said, 'Congratulations.' She hesitated for a moment and laughingly asked, 'Why are you congratulating me?' He responded, 'You're going to have a baby.' She was stunned, as she had just recently learned that she was indeed pregnant and had told no one.*

***T**hey were expecting a baby and didn't want to know whether it was a boy or a girl. The doctor wrote the gender of the baby on a sheet of paper in his own script, folded it, and gave it to them. They put the paper away and never looked at it.*

One night he dreamt he saw the paper unfold and saw the gender of their baby written in a beautiful script. He told his wife of the dream, but not what he had read. When their baby daughter was born, they looked at the paper, and in the same beautiful script written by the doctor were the words, 'It's a Girl,' exactly as he had seen it in his dream.

Her husband was murdered; a senseless act of violence of teens under the influence of drugs. What was significant is that a few days earlier, he dreamt of being with an old friend of his mother-in-law's. He wondered why she appeared in his dream, why they were communicating and sharing an experience together. They subsequently learned that she died approximately the same time he was killed.

He was diagnosed with terminal cancer and given a few months to live. During his final weeks, he was having dreams about people who had crossed over. What was confusing is that one of the individuals was still living. They both died on the same day. I subconsciously logged all those instances, thinking one day I was going to make sense of them.

The following is a dream in reverse, where one who had died and was buried was asking for help from one who was living. If souls continue how could he be in the ground? In time understanding did come. Somehow, it always does.

Her husband had just been buried. In a dream she saw him shivering. He told her he was very cold, that he was being covered by water and needed her help. The following morning remembering her dream, she went to his plot and saw that a hose had not been turned off, and cold water was running into her husband's freshly dug grave.

These dreams, among many that were shared, offered me the opportunity to believe that this form of communication often enables us to see and connect with people and events from the past, present, and future. How special it is not to feel disconnected with all our loved ones.

"Miracles happen to those who believe in them."

Bernard Berenson

Chapter Fifteen
A Miracle

I had to be a pillar of strength for our families. My daughter-in-law was gone, and I had to keep my emotions tightly contained within with no outward show of emotion. We were all grieving. I stifled any sobs fearing if I would lose control they all would, unraveling the final thread holding all our lives together.

How was I to keep myself together? My soul was screaming; not a sound was heard. I was drowning; not a tear fell. They had been together 19 of their 38 years, but had no time to say goodbye, to speak words to each other that would matter ... *always remember how much I love you ... I'm sorry if I ever hurt you.*

I wanted to be strong enough to help my son take the steps necessary to fulfill new dreams he would choose in time; for her parents to learn to bring their grief and unhappiness inside; and for my granddaughters to learn that the love they shared with their mother would bridge the time between them and last throughout Eternity.

I prayed long and hard wanting and waiting to be heard ... waiting for a direction. Then, without warning, a miracle happened, although not anything I would have imagined.

***D**uring a trip to my sister's condo in upstate New York, I drove to one of the largest spiritualist assemblies in the United States. Six dollars gave me entry into a community I didn't understand. It was the first time I had ever attended, and I was excited with the possibility of meeting my loved ones in spirit. Things aren't that simple, and they happen when they're meant to happen.*

I didn't know what to expect or what to do with my time there. Despite the fact that I wasn't really a believer of the healing of TV evangelists, I decided to go to a healing temple where individuals dressed in white were using a spiritual healing procedure called 'hands-on healing.'

What I saw were individuals with crutches and canes going to a healer for prayers. What was I doing there? I sat on a bench looking and thinking, and recalled a similar event that took place in 1981 while living in New York City.

Having heard of a healing session taking place on the westside of Manhattan, I decided to attend. Upon entering I took a seat on the sofa, closed my eyes and listened to Pachelbel's 'Kanon in D.' Within a few minutes I burst into tears and was immediately directed to lay down on a table surrounded by six people dressed in white. I was told I needed healing and asked what I wanted healed.

In the process of getting a divorce, I asked for my legs to be healed. There was nothing wrong with my legs, but I felt as a mother and single parent of five children I needed a strong foundation to be able to provide the best care for my children.

The woman standing over me at the head of the table, who appeared to be the leader, responded that it was my heart that needed healing to support me through the grief I would be facing in the near future. Although I didn't understand it, I didn't question what she had said, and they proceeded with the hands-on healing session. I thanked them and left wondering if or what I should be feeling.

Time passed and a few months later I was at a friend's home to which a Tarot reader had been invited. Tarot, a pack of playing cards used from the mid-15th century, reveals the present and future. He asked to give me a reading, and I agreed. Connecting with my vibration, the reader told me I would soon be facing a tragedy in my life. I thanked him and was once again left wondering what I was supposed to be feeling.

Was there any truth to the messages I was being told? Twice, not once! There was definitely a thread connecting the two sessions, but I couldn't see it. It was that December that my son died.

Over 15 years had passed and here I was back in a similar situation. When the healing temple was about to close with only a few of us remaining, I decided to walk toward the front and sit in a chair. The healer asked me what I wanted healed, and I replied, 'my heart.'

Proceeding with hands-on healing, I quickly became engulfed in heat from a brilliant light cascading through the stained glass window not far from where I was seated. I felt embraced by the rays of the sun and felt tranquil. I couldn't think; I didn't want to think; I just wanted to continue feeling bathed in the extraordinary light.

When the procedure was over, I fumbled a thank you and left. By the time I returned to the condo, it didn't take me long to realize that I could bend the ring finger of my left hand. This may not sound like a miracle to you, but that finger had been broken, and following surgery and months of physical therapy, I had been told I would never be able to fully bend my finger again. And yet, here it was five years later, and I could; I was ... just like that. I didn't know what had happened or why it happened; I just knew that something extraordinary and miraculous had occurred.

God's spiritual healing can best be explained as an invisible life force in the universe. This energy, also called *prana* or *qi*, not only healed my finger, but also my heart. I believe it was a way of letting me know not to lose faith, that God would help me, would help all of us get through this period that was stifling us and breaking our hearts. I didn't lose faith, and that power of faith has remained with me.

Shortly thereafter I developed a strong interest in energy medicine and alternative healing practices using touch. I attended sessions on reflexology, acupressure, chiropractic medicine, and Ayurveda, India's 5,000 year-old natural system of healing which treats the individual as a whole. This is much like the teachings of Hippocrates, a Greek physician considered the Father of Medicine, and in whose philosophy I had been raised.

Spiritual healing is always possible. One day some form of energy medicine will present itself to each of us, whether or not we seek it, whether or not we ask for it. It's the way of the future.

"There are only two ways to live your life. One is as though nothing is a miracle - the other is as though everything is a miracle."
(Albert Einstein)

... More than the heart can bear is unhappiness remembering happiness.

... *C*ome back. Even as a shadow, even as a dream.

(Euripides)

*"I love you in this way
because I do not know any other
way of loving but this,
in which there is no I or you..."*

Pablo Neruda

Chapter Sixteen
*The **P**assing **O**f Time*

I arrived at the beach early that day. The morning mist had not yet lifted. The sky was gray, but the sun was strong, even at that hour, burning off the haze and already beginning to burn my skin. I applied some suntan lotion, something I rarely do, to protect me from what? I had been pierced so many times by grief, nothing else could harm me, and I didn't care if it did.

The waves were gently rolling in, getting closer to my blanket. I wonder if I had misjudged the level of high tide, which was to peak at 9:57 am. The seagulls were chattering, walking the beach, skimming the water, while others soared above presumably seeking to make their exclamation. Two boats were out in the distance, sailing where the ocean meets the sky, perhaps fishing because they appeared fixed in their position. Only one lone boat was actually sailing across the horizon, one which for whatever reason chose a different direction. It made me wonder whether or not we also have control over our direction in life. Did my daughter-in-law?

There were already a few people on the jetty and an umbrella or two on the beach. Two families had their babies in the refreshing water, and an elderly couple sat in their sand chairs wearing their hats and sunglasses. The way they were looking at each other with love brought tears to my eyes. How wonderful it would be if my son would be able to feel that way again.

The sand was filled with the usual array of broken shells, beach pebbles polished smoothly, some seaweed and usual debris, including cigarette butts in the sand. The only thing marring this tranquil state was the occasional sand flea pecking at my legs and feet, reminding me of the frailty and pain that can easily be inflicted on us when life appears to be at its best. They are deceiving appearances in life. What may be peaceful can be turbulent; what may be here one moment, without warning not here the next.

A Spanish couple was edging into the water to feel its coolness before diving in. I am always amazed at how fast the Spanish language is spoken, and years of studying Spanish in school were not helping me understand what it was they were saying that was so funny. And I needed to laugh … especially that day.

It was no ordinary day. I had gone down to the water early that morning because it was the one year passing of my daughter-in-law, long before her time, long before she was ready. She loved the beach, and I wanted to feel close to her. Simply, I wanted her back.

I would have been playing with the boys had they not succumbed with her. My granddaughter had named them even though they were five months old in utero when they passed on. Why do I think I know them? Why do I hurt not having them here if I never really knew them? Are we so connected in others' lives that our memory does not fail us completely, but allows us to recall those we've met in our past lives or will meet in future ones? Maybe I had known them.

On occasion my granddaughter talked about her brothers. *If they were here, they would be toddling around.* I believe children have a sensitivity, an intuition that makes them more receptive than adults to see through the invisible veil separating time.

I also believe it is true of animals. When my daughter-in-law died, her cat went into the basement where I would feed her daily, and no amount of coaxing from any of us would get her to come upstairs into the house. Why did she choose that week to emerge into the light above from the darkness of the basement where she had remained since my daughter-in-law's death? Having mourned her for one year, it was time for her to move on. Her cat walked through the house, and as if saying goodbye made the decision and ... died.

My son was still experiencing anguish from his loss, and maybe this was a signal for him to move on and save his two daughters, whose lives had not yet been lived and whose joys were prematurely cut short by their mother's passing. An injustice had been done. I was there, and his wife wasn't; I was mothering his children, and his wife wasn't.

Our journey continues, and new decisions are faced. My son's and daughter-in-law's lives came to a temporary abrupt halt. What was their path? She was meant to continue with their two little boys, and he with their two little girls. Their journey continued; their equation changed.

There were times when I thought it was meant to be. Why else did my path take a turn, and I lived with them for three months prior to her death? If I was going to teach that summer on Cape Cod, I would have found a place to live. Yet I couldn't motivate myself, and as a result, I was available to be near them and with them from the onset of this devastating period upon their lives, upon our family.

Life had been in emotional turmoil since my daughter-in-law's passing. I needed to do something that was normal to verify my existence beyond the past, which seemed so very long ago instead of only a year. I had to find a way to move forward, and remembering energy healing and the miracle that occurred, I began to study Reiki, a Japanese hands-on technique for stress reduction and relaxation that also promotes healing.

By coincidence, my son was studying Reiki at the same time. We lived in the same house; neither knew what the other was doing, yet both of us were in the same vibration, choosing this alternative mode of healing at the very same time. Going through this process somehow, eventually and unconsciously, enabled us to heal each other.

"Doubt is a pain too lonely to know that faith is his twin brother."

Khalil Gibran

Chapter Seventeen
Interfacing With The Spirit World

I was born in Brooklyn, New York, where I spent the first 14 years of my life. On occasion my father would take me with him when he went to see what he called gypsies, presently referred to as mediums and psychics.

Mediums have fine-tuned their sixth sense to interface with spirits in other dimensions. They are known to be sensitive and receptive to higher frequencies from other than themselves and have the ability to see, feel, and hear voices from those in the spirit world.

As a young adult in New York City I would coax my friends to come with me to see psychics. I was always told about my future, never thinking of asking them to try connecting me with individuals who had died, not that I really knew of any … until later in life.

A number of times seeking solace I would visit the spiritualist village in upstate New York oftentimes wanting to see the mediums in residence. I would peruse the board where their names were listed and choose one whose name resonated with me at the time. There was no logic, just an intuition, a sixth sense that can't be explained.

    During my very first visit while sitting among a hundred or so people, I was called upon by the medium at the front of the small amphitheater. I was told to speak clearly to enable the vibration of my voice to resonate with the individual in the spirit world seeking to contact me.

    It was my father. How did I know? At first I didn't. Many things the medium had said were familiar to me except one - that my father had died with a tube in his throat. I didn't believe her, although I really didn't know because my father had died while staying with my sister. When I later contacted my sister, she told me it was true.

How appropriate that my father should be the first person in spirit to present himself to me. He was the one who believed and taught me that individuals can communicate with those who have crossed over. He called them gypsies. That's who they were in the village in Greece where he was born and raised and who were his best friends.

At that visit I was also connected with my son. I knew immediately that it was he because the words the medium spoke were the exact words he and I shared prior to his crossing over. I knew it was not coincidental. It wasn't anything she pieced together waiting for some validation from me. She would have no way of knowing what we had intimately spoken about unless they were shared with her by my son. This was the last time I disbelieved what I didn't understand.

For no particular reason other than curiosity, he went to see a medium. While she spoke he made certain not to respond in any manner, nor show any emotion at what she was saying from which she could possibly glean information to continue her reading. She told him that he and his wife were expecting a baby; indeed they had recently learned the wonderful news; and that a man with the initial 'G' was watching over his son until his birth and not to worry. At that time he did not know they were expecting a boy, however, he indeed knew of someone in his family with the initial 'G' who had crossed over. His son was born on 'G's' birthday. Coincidental?

The medium also shared a vision with him in which his deceased brother in the spirit world told him that he was honored his name was being considered as a middle name for his unborn child if it were to be a boy. That was exactly what he and his wife had discussed … if they were to have a boy, they would give him his brother's name as a middle name. Life is truly mysterious.

It was a simple tupperware party to which she invited a group of friends. To entertain them, she invited a medium to give some readings. She was not a believer, at least not at the time, nor did she know the woman. When it was her turn for a reading, she was told that she and her family would soon be flying out of state, have a house full of people upon their return, and the name of one important individual would have the initial 'B.'

She laughed at what had been said. In no uncertain terms was she planning to have a group of people stay at her home, and she knew no one whose name began with the letter 'B!' Especially amusing to hear was that she and her family would be taking a flight. They had never flown anywhere, nor did they intend to. How ludicrous it all sounded.

It was soon thereafter that her heart was pierced. Her sister whom she loved dearly had died suddenly. It was my daughter-in-law's death. The entire family flew out of state to be with her, to have some closure to the unexpected abrupt ending of one they loved.

Upon their return, her home was filled with friends who had come for her sister's memorial service. The name of the one guest closest to her sister's husband who lived a few thousand miles away began with the letter 'B.' How can it all be explained except to say if you're open to mystical experiences, you will have them.

There were many incidences that took place over a period of a few visits to the spiritualist community; each one true; each one memorable; and too many to write about. However, it continued to verify for me that time and space do not exist except in our minds.

We are all here, present and accounted for.

*"Prayer is when you talk to God;
meditation is when you listen to God."*

Author Unknown

Chapter Eighteen
Walking The Labyrinth

We follow different paths, straight or crooked, and end our lives where we were initially heading. God has carried me throughout numerous trials in my life, even though I may have been more liberal than most perhaps allowing my free will full reign in choosing directions.

No matter how difficult or easy, big or small, I find myself praying to God with prayers of *please, help me, tell me what to do, thank you.* Although my choices haven't always been acceptable to others, I have never had the sense that God has disapproved. God has been and remains my guiding force … my GPS.

There are times when I question the term spiritual energy for no reason other than that it's new to me. It is easier, however, to validate knowing that the universe operates through a dynamic exchange of giving and receiving, and everything that is in vibrational harmony with our focus comes to us. Simply, what goes around, comes around.

We become what we think, and I try to think positively, visualize and send my vibration into the universe with the hope and expectation that it will come back to me in the same way. The silence causes me to focus and is helpful with my meditation and prayer. It works for me. Does this sound too simple?

Neuroscientific studies show that meditation can change brain chemistry, and being mindful can help restructure our brain by changing negative to positive. Becoming mindful of our actions and in our prayers cause them to multiply in the same manner, and they are paid forward in time.

I both meditate and pray, especially in those all-important moments in time when I feel I need to be heard … perhaps more importantly that I will hear … and to which response I will listen; much the same as when I walk the labyrinth.

I have walked labyrinths many times in numerous locations. I seek them out because each time they leave me feeling emotionally uplifted and always with a sense of calm and peace. I liken the walk to a spiritual journey and feel a mind/body/spirit connection.

Although a labyrinth looks like a maze, it isn't. There are no dead ends. It has a well-defined circuitous path that winds its way into the center and back out again on the same path. Walking the labyrinth is an exercise that allows me to quietly focus internally, to center myself and allow prayer and reflection without interference. It is safe and inspiring.

On the way to the center, I release thoughts that may be troubling me. Reaching the center I stop to pray, and on the way out, I receive thoughts - some in answer to my concerns and some about which I should be thinking. I guess it's like crossing over and bringing back into this world what we have learned. Can we call this miraculous?

Walking the labyrinth is the ability to listen to our subconscious, to our inner self, intuitively, and then telepathically listen to an answer. This response comes from an inner voice, from a form of intelligence beyond rational thought, beyond the rational mind, from God within.

I recall the first time I introduced meditation to my seven-year old granddaughter when I brought her with me to walk a labyrinth. I tried to explain to her what it means to be mindful, especially mindful while walking the labyrinth, concentrating on sharing what was on her mind and in her heart. This was difficult to understand for one so young, but I truly believe when the time is right there is understanding. And it was for her. Although only seven, she was ready.

Her mother had passed away when she was only 18 months old. Her mother always had her close to her, like an appendage, and one day was suddenly gone, disappearing from her life.

My granddaughter would look at her mother's car in the garage and run around the house calling for her … *Mama … Mama …* and there was never a response. She searched for six months.

My heart was breaking. Her mother was her life-line, and she was confused for a long time at losing her - questioning where she was. She wanted an answer and needed to keep her mother's memory with her. I couldn't bear it any longer, and one day I told her that her mother was in heaven, that she would always be in her heart, near her, hear her, and someday she may be able to do the same.

Was that too much information? All I knew is that I needed to comfort her as compassionately and as honestly as possible. That night she came into my bed, and curling up in my arms in a fetal position cried for over three hours. We both cried. I didn't know how she, I, we would ever get through this trauma. From that day forward she stopped calling out her mother's name, and spoke very little for sometime thereafter. Was the shock too much for her?

Although surrounded by family I wondered if a child that age could feel abandonment; how long she would remember the image of her mother. I didn't have long to wait. Throughout her toddler years whenever we were in situations with young mothers and their children, she would gravitate toward a mother that resembled her own, throw her arms tightly around the mother's legs and not let go.

Although perplexed, the young mothers were always kind, allowing her those moments, and I would later explain to them of the sudden death of her mother. Sixteen years later she continues to seek information about her mother … what she was like … what they did together … an affirmation - a reaffirmation that she was real.

The reason she agreed to join me in walking the labyrinth is that she felt her family didn't approve of her spontaneous behavior of which she had no control or understanding and was looking for guidance.

At the labyrinth she listened carefully to what I had to say. I watched her walk slowly with her hands clasped together in front of her as if in prayer, unlike her usual behavior because she was a highly energetic child, always running and jumping. Upon reaching the center she stopped. Standing there for what seemed to me to be a very long time, I then heard her say, *'I'm praying to you, God, to please, please, help me be good.'*

Was I too wrapped up in my own sorrow at the time and missed her cry for help? Were her outbursts a result of internal anger, confusion, frustration? If they were, I unknowingly failed her and in turn failed in my promise to my daughter-in-law that I would always watch out for her daughters. I'll never know. Maybe I don't want to know.

The precious gifts of affection and love don't cost anything, and are often the most difficult to give. But not for this granddaughter of mine, my second, who is one of the purest souls in my life. She does not have a mean bone in her body. She exudes happiness and makes everyone around her happy. To this day, she pays it forward with kindness and love, and it returns to her a hundred-fold.

I believe this childlike love leads to a universal love of all there is, known and unknown. And what else is there? What else matters? To love and be loved unconditionally, eternally.

When a loved one who has died appears before you, it's not your heart that fights it, it's your brain. When someone is in your heart, they're never truly gone. They can come back to you, even at unlikely times. The two worlds are not so far apart. You can dream of them, bring them to mind, and your thoughts may bring them to you.

"...And live like it's heaven on earth."

William W. Purkey

Chapter Nineteen
Heaven On Earth

During my son's last month of life, we sat in the family room talking together about what he could be facing. I was living in intense agony and grief that I would soon be losing him, and at the same time denying that it would ever really happen.

My son, however, never denied it, and unlike his usual behavior he began to treat his siblings in an angry manner. When I asked him why he was behaving that way, he said that if they began to hate him, they wouldn't miss him when he was gone. We spent hours talking about the quality of life … his and of those he loved.

Realizing how little time he had, he decided to leave something of his for each of his siblings to remember him by and began drawing birthday cards for me to give to them the following year when he would no longer be with them. He was so thoughtful and mature for his age … profoundly wise … a sage.

When his life was ebbing, he began to journey beyond this life to the next. He kept crossing over, although I did not use that term at the time, and began to share with me what he was experiencing, much of which I did not understand at the time, nor for many years thereafter. He wasn't dreaming, and he couldn't be hallucinating. He was not in any pain, and he was not on any medication. Simply and tragically, his heart was failing and he was coming to terms with what lay ahead of him.

He told me of his communication with others who had crossed over, family he did not know, but who I recognized by his description; people that were in the room with all of us; visible only to him. Why couldn't I see them?

At the time I couldn't understand how he was connecting with them. Where were they? How did they appear? Where was he? He told me that he saw beautiful trees and flowers, a place that was sunny and warm, where rain fell but never touched you, where sickness and disability did not exist, where he felt happy and protected. It wasn't until years later that I realized my own mind was limiting me from seeing and believing.

I now often use the term crossing over. Its significance was something I did not fully understand at the time. Somehow we lift the veil that separates us, and we're able to see and think while crossing over in time.

"Faith is a passionate intuition."
(William Wordsworth)

A close friend of mine is religious and spiritual with an inherent faith that everything will work out, and for as long as I've known him, it does. One evening he had poor visibility driving home during a snow storm. He skidded off the highway onto a very steep secondary mountain road, unplowed and slippery. Trying to maneuver the car from veering off onto an embankment, he found himself praying to God for help.

He kept building up speed as he was spiraling downward. Having no control of his car, he took his hands off the wheel, and said to God that he was releasing himself into His hands. The car flew with the speed of a luge for what seemed to him to be forever, and stopped suddenly in a clearing not far from the main street of a small town. What/who had guided him?

She was driving on a major highway during a snow storm when she was hit from behind by a skidding van that pummeled her off a steep embankment. Although she was in shock, and only a few seconds in time had passed, she began praying that she was leaving everything in His hands. As her car careened, soaring downward across tree tops, she sensed the nearness of her husband who had died years before, telling her she would be all right, and she felt the car being carried to a lofty landing in a tree.

Her battered car nestled in a tree hanging halfway down the long steep embankment. Travelers on the highway had left their cars on the side of the road to see what assistance they could give. Thinking the worst, that she had died, they were shocked at what they saw. Graced by God, she was found trembling, unscathed, without a scratch.

Having faith and the power of prayer is nothing short of miraculous.

On the day of my ex husband's funeral, for reasons unclear to me I was not to attend. But let me begin a few days earlier. I was traveling from Florida to Georgia to visit my daughters for the Martin Luther King commemorative weekend. While in flight, I had a strong sensation and vivid picture that he was being moved to Hospice after a year-long debilitating stay in a hospital. I was overcome with grief ... saddened that life had brought him down a tragic path, and at the same time I was somehow untroubled because I sensed that he would now be free to choose to die when he was ready.

When I arrived I told my daughters what I had seen and felt. The next morning they received a phone call letting them know that their father had died in Hospice. He died leaning on his elbow, looking out the window at the sea which he loved. He chose his time and died with dignity, love, and peace.

For reasons beyond my understanding or control, I was asked not to attend and remained at my daughter's home as the families flew to the funeral. I was filled with sadness, grief, shock. I was alone, and I was distraught that I had been denied a chance for closure. I walked around the house crying at his passing, recalling our happy memories and years together, thinking of the magnitude of his loss to his children and grandchildren.

I sat on the edge of my daughter's bed sobbing. Out of the corner of my eye I saw what appeared to be a sheet of paper at the top of the bureau that slowly began floating back and forth down toward me, landing face up beside me on the bed. I was shaken. What I saw was a photo of my deceased son smiling up at me, as if saying, everything's all right. I am here. And I cried even harder.

This was obviously a sign, a message sent to me to calm me down. Where did it come from? Sent by whom? My ex-husband? My son? Were both father and son together? Were they with me? The how was unimportant. I stopped questioning and thought, of course they were together; of course they were with me; there is no separation of time and space.

When signs appear to us, who is to question the occurrences that we cannot yet understand. I find it meaningful to accept what is presented, until one day proven impossible or one day proven true.

I had never heard of near-death research during the time I was grieving, nor of Elizabeth Kubler Ross, psychiatrist, author, and pioneer in near-death studies.

The information my son shared with me resulted from what he had learned from repeated personal experiences he had while crossing over during the last month of his life.

"Invest ... in acquiring knowledge for yourself ... and ... you keep your children and grandchildren and unborn generations enlightened by what you have already learned!"

Israelmore Ayivor

Chapter Twenty
The Continuation Of Life

It is believed in many churches that the body of a deceased remains on earth for 40 days before ascending into heaven.

Upon returning to Florida after Mama's funeral, my sister and I saw that the poinsettia bush Mama had planted *outside her back door had grown over six feet tall. We couldn't understand how that could have happened. It was only two feet tall three weeks earlier. We both strongly felt that was Mama's way of telling us she was still around.*

After Mama's passing, I was trying to figure out what to do, where to go. I had been living with her for two years and now the silence made it difficult for me to be there without her. I knew I had to move on; I just didn't know where. What I didn't want was to feel that I had to do what everyone else wanted me to do, but instead do what I wanted, what was best for me. Does it matter what everyone else thinks, or does it matter what we think?

One evening, I walked in the front door, sat in the chair she had by the entrance and began to cry. I had a difficult day trying to sort out my life and make some choices. I wasn't ready to move on. When I turned on the light, I saw Mama's beautiful purple flowers strewn all over the floor leading into the kitchen, her favorite room. That morning they were in a vase on the dining room table. How could that be? How could they have gotten out of the vase?

Most people would need to find a rational explanation, but there was none. I believe my mother wanted me to know that she was there, and that everything would be fine going forward. It was so like her to worry about me. At that moment I loved her more deeply than ever. For all the times we were unable to say that to one another, I hoped she had heard my thoughts and knew.

From what I had heard and subsequently believed is that when you die, there is wonderful beauty and light, and when you go through the light you become part of that energy forever. You are no longer a limited being. You are a spirit without a physical form.

Our lives come before us in a fast-forward motion as a life review for resolution before we cross over, and we begin to understand the reasons for every decision made and every action taken that have affected all our intertwined lives. As Mama drew near death, she didn't speak and looked perplexed. It was obvious by her expression that a lot was going on that she couldn't understand and caused her angst.

In her later years Mama had difficulty hearing and perhaps thought she couldn't hear or understand what was being said, unaware that every communication is done telepathically. I can imagine how the experience leading up to her passing, even during her passing, could overwhelm and frighten her. As strong as she could be, she seemed underneath it all to be very fragile. I wondered who was going to help her cross over or who would be meeting her.

Mama always had a special relationship with her first granddaughter, who was at her home at the time of Mama's death. She was overwhelmed with grief, strongly sensing that her Yiayia had died. She had just left her less than two hours before. Why hadn't she stayed longer? That's when she felt her presence next to her. Her beloved Yiayia had come to see her and say goodbye. The love between them knew no boundaries, enabling her to help her Yiayia cross over. I never asked my daughter what she had seen or what they had said to each other. It was a special private moment between them. The love and support they were giving each other was theirs alone.

My mother was very close to her first great grandson. They both shared an extra special bond of love. He was a toddler when she crossed over. One day when he was two he went rummaging through the drawer in his mother's bedside table. When asked what he was doing, he responded that his great grandmother, whom he also called Yiayia, had once given him a birthday card that was never opened. It contained money for ice cream, which was her custom, and had been told by her that it was in his mother's bedroom in the top drawer of her nightstand.

His mother emptied the contents of the drawer on her bed, and they began looking for the card together. It indeed was a birthday card given to him in which there were a couple of dollars with a note that said simply, 'this is for you to buy some ice cream.'

When my grandson was standing on a stool at the kitchen counter waiting to help wash the dishes, his mother cautioned him to be careful not to fall backwards. He turned around to look behind him, and then looking back at his mother told her in no uncertain terms that he couldn't/wouldn't fall because his Yiayia was behind him watching over him.

It's not easy finding a reason … a rational one … but easy if you believe. His Yiayia was with him. We are all together if we allow ourselves to see without blinders, without allowing ourselves to be swayed in thought because we're unsure or because others don't understand. That doesn't mean it isn't so. It doesn't mean it can't be so.

Once you stop making death an uncomfortable subject and stop torturing yourself, you can begin accepting that there is in fact no separation of time. There is not even a lapse of consciousness. It's just a matter of closing your eyes in one dimension and opening them in another. It's wonderful believing that something so beautiful simply happens, and you're no longer afraid.

I have seen people become relaxed before death and share vivid experiences with deceased loved ones. Often when people are dying they hold on to life hoping to see their loved ones one last time. Over the years I've had conversations with various people who told me what they had heard from their loved ones during the last days of their lives. The stories were all similar.

She would visit her brother daily in the hospital during the last week of his life. On the day before he died, he described to her that he had seen how beautiful it was where he was going - beautiful trees, colors, flowers - a place that gave him a sense of peace and calm. She didn't know what to make of it, thinking he must have been hallucinating. It wasn't until I shared similar experiences with her did she realize it could have been true.

Her husband was sitting with us at the table, and he began to tell us about his own brother who had been in his final stages. He had also visited him on his last day and had been told the very same thing his wife had just shared. This couple had been living together for almost 50 years and neither had ever mentioned it to the other.

There will be times when the opportunity will arise to share your story. Don't be afraid that you'll be rejected or ridiculed. The time you feel it is the right time to do so. You'll stop thinking that you may be crazy and begin to feel relief at having expressed a long kept secret. To have stories confirmed brings affirmation and a sense of peace.

How can all these people crossing over share similar experiences … finding themselves no longer in pain … going from a place of darkness into one of light … going from non being into being?

The answer for me is that it can only be made possible by the power of One who has always existed.

Life is so beautifully unpredictable.

> *"...long have you timidly waded*
> *holding a plank by the shore.*
> *...now I 'will' you to be a bold swimmer,*
> *to jump off in the midst of the sea,*
> *rise again, nod to me. Shout."*
>
> Walt Whitman

Chapter Twenty One
A New Beginning

She had walked into my son's life, and somehow we all knew that she belonged there. Her death was so tragic ... senseless. Grief was part of our lives as an uncontrollable emotion that was controlled only to help us move on. I hoped for a miracle that would make this bottled up sadness go away.

When my son's wife died he was broken. Her love was pressed in him forever, and his life revolved around the moment he lost her. Knowing that in some corner of his being there would always be an ache of longing, my son also knew that he had to love again, not only for his daughters, but because he would die completely.

By what means would he be able to embrace his suffering and come to terms with his grief; when he could smile when someone said something funny; or joke within family settings that brought up memories of loved ones and laughter? With all the chatter of the girls, his silence was deafening. He was distraught. I was confused. Our eyes did not meet. Any attempt at communication was returned by a look and an occasional written note. The more I despaired, the more ineffective I became. I had to learn to live as if he were a ghost making appearances in the home we shared without uttering a sound.

How could I read his soul to understand what he wanted, what he needed? All I knew is that to survive he had to move on with someone who could love and comfort him, someone who would provide mothering to his girls, someone who was not his mother. Someday, someone would find a place in my son's heart … never in the same way, never with the same intensity of pledged eternal love; differently, so there would not be any comparisons.

As much as I tried to help him, I was playing both roles, losing myself in both, feeling ineffective in both. All I could do was pray, *Please, God, help him.* He had to find the answer to his own salvation.

Where there is hope and faith, through prayer there are miracles. Death doesn't just take someone, it also misses someone, and the distance between being taken and being missed changes our life. My son had to move on with a singular purpose - to survive and take care of his two daughters.

Many people are unable to survive such a tragedy. He did. He knew he had to change for all of them to survive, and he prayed for guidance. My son was blessed and was granted Grace. In that one moment of Grace something powerful and special occurred that changed his life forever. He was given the vision to put his life back together, and that vision presented to him was religion.

Science and religion merged, and that opened the door to a new beginning, not in terms of someone, but something. He registered in the divinity school associated with the university in New Haven where he worked as a neuroscientist, immersing himself completely into working in the lab, attending classes, and caring for his daughters. I was beginning to feel hope that he would at last come to terms with the tragedy of losing his first and only love.

I began to believe that when one door closes, another one does open because it did. Little by little enthusiasm and laughter re-entered his life, and solace was found as he was turning his life around. The choice was his alone and from a neuroscientist he became a priest. Oftentimes Grace and miracles cannot be perceived as being possible. You need to believe they are possible and most importantly acknowledge them when they do happen.

My son was doubly blessed. At divinity school he met a woman who shared similar professional accomplishments, as he in science and religion, she in medicine and religion. There is a higher power, I thought, listening to our prayers, and responding with love. This was a new beginning for all of us, and our lives began to slowly change as we moved on to new adventures.

A new companion entered my son's life to fill his longing for a mother to his daughters. Although their journey held difficult years, they were blessed with two children, a boy and a girl, and their life's journey continued.

Initially, in his grief, when my son stood at this major crossroad in his life, he could not see the possibilities before him.

However, his prayers were heard and answered, and my son was blessed. The choice he made opened a door to a way of life he had never envisioned.

Happiness has now re-entered the lives of my granddaughters who were four-years old and 18 months old at the time, and are now recent graduates of college and high school respectively.

My son learned the value of spiritual peace. He has vision and imagination and the energy to give 110% to his new direction and expanded ministry. Through creative programming he reaches out to all people; brings church to them; helps them renew and/or enhance their faith and live it in their own context; inspires them to rid themselves of despair by helping them believe that everything is possible with hope ... and hope requires having faith.

There's no end to what he can do, and will do, and while doing so, it may be possible for him to bring understanding to the merging of the great challenge of religion and science to the minds of humankind. Prayers do get heard and answered, and whether or not we're aware of it, our GPS is always in motion. Life is miraculous!

*"Darkness cannot drive out darkness:
only light can do that."*

Martin Luther King, Jr.

Chapter Twenty Two
A Final Goodbye

The hardest encounter in my life was now before me, and I prayed. My son was Graced in October, and I was still not ready to let him go. How much time did we have together? I felt the power of my prayers kept him with me, and if you can understand this, I believe his staying with me was also of his choosing trying to help me.

One afternoon as we sat together, we talked in depth about the ebbing of his life. I felt I owed him that honesty. He listened and told me that it was something he already knew, but everyone was afraid to talk about it with him, pretending that nothing was going to happen, denying that he was actually going to die.

How hard it was for me to hear those words from him. He was my child. This should not be happening. He felt it was now finally possible for him to talk about what he was going through, what was going to happen to him. The conversations between us made it possible for him to share with me all that he was experiencing.

Sometimes we're so terrified watching our loved ones die that instead of sharing our last moments together and being present in that moment, we run the other way. Unable to live with that reality, we live on the cusp, crazy with denial and fear.

We go to bed scared and wake up scared, knowing they walk around at night for the same reason. And when they hold on, and life goes on, we get to believe they're never going to die, and when they do we're still in denial.

The understanding that we were looking at the inevitable together created an extra special bond between us. We both acknowledged that he was dying, but we didn't talk about it. *When* was not part of the equation; what we were able to do *now* to enjoy the present was.

Thanksgiving was upon us. My son was a great little chef and was looking forward to cooking for this family gathering. The day of thanksgiving, however, brought us sadness. We felt blessed that he was with us, however, he was unable to endure the aromas of all his favorite dishes being prepared. I cried trying not to think of what we would be facing, consumed with the horror of what would soon eventually happen. *Please God, not yet.*

It was early December. My son and I were seated together in a large chair in the family room. Around three in the afternoon as he was talking about his experiences, we heard the sound of the school bus stopping at our driveway.

The front door opened, and his siblings entered the house. He asked me if they were home, and when I responded *yes,* he said, *Mom, I have to go now. Okay?* He knew through my prayers that I had not been ready to let him go, but he was suffering, and staying alive was too difficult for him. I couldn't hold on to him forever, and before I finished saying *yes,* he was gone.

How could I have said *yes,* never to have him near me again, never to hold him, hug him and kiss him. My son was gone and a part of me died with him. We don't fear our own death as much as we fear the death of the ones we love. The shock of death is emotional not only to the heart but to the mind. I never forgave myself. It was never again to be *no more* which would have left me with some hope; it was a definitive *yes.*

We can sometimes spend years, decades, overcoming the fact that they are no longer with us, no matter how much we have prepared ourselves for their death. No matter how much we did or didn't do, we think of hundreds of things we could have done or said. But we all do what we're capable of doing, which is to hold on to our own salvation, and after a while, we get used to the sorrows heaped upon our heart.

Years later I look back as if it were yesterday and wonder if I had been stronger could I have reversed reality? But I couldn't have. The choice was his to make, and when it was time for him to make it, he did.

My life was touched by an enormous tragedy, and I fell into a black hole. There was pain in my home, in my heart, a pain that didn't stop, that wouldn't go away. What purpose did all of this have? My son was in control, and then he wasn't. Or was he? Wasn't he the one who said it was time for me to release him? I loved him more than ever, but I couldn't let my love and grief hold him. I had to say *yes* so he could move on. I had to let him go for his sake.

Following his death, making funeral arrangements was painful. My son loved horses, and his father and I had chosen a plot a few months earlier, one that overlooked a pasture with horses running free. That was difficult … having to make that decision while our son was still alive. However, arrangements made upon his death were even more difficult … choosing the coffin which would hold the body of our young son.

What was unexpected was the degree of other people's involvement with the funeral arrangements. I had a difficult time trying not to resent their interference. They were well-meaning, I guess, choosing to help in that way, or they felt it was their responsibility to take over at a time of grief. How could I have made them understand that the one thing worse than a child dying on you is to have him eventually … die.

I wanted to be alone with him, without their interference, without the decisions they were making for me. Did they not know this was a process, a closure, I had to go through? Did they think they were sparing me, or sparing themselves by easing their own pain?

I had to begin to learn how to live without him, to be happy that he went on as a free soul, and to stop wishing my turn would come to enter that dark passage into the light to see him and be with him. It's hard for those of us left behind, left alone to endure life without the one we love. We may adjust to the loss, but we never get over it. We never forget.

My children. How was I going to help my children find some understanding? I couldn't. I failed them when they needed me most. I was consumed only with the one that was no longer with me. Mama had done the same thing when my brother died, and I resented it, yet I was doing the same thing. *God, please don't let me lose them.*

Time heals. We don't think it will, but it does. My children healed, and I could not have healed without them. I love them unconditionally and will be forever thankful for all they have given me and for always being there for me. The tables were reversed, and I was learning from them. I don't think I will ever understand why I happen to be so blessed, however, what I do know is that I will be forever grateful.

Many wonder if there is ever any consolation for those left behind. For me, solace came in remembering what my son shared with me about crossing over - *that there is a painless life into the light toward which they travel, where everything is peaceful, where loved ones who have crossed over wait for us.* The spirit, the soul, is free of all human physical limitations in time and space. I so wanted it to be true. I so needed it to be true in order to make some sense of this tragedy.

Sometimes we look for mystical answers. If there is no other life for our loved ones, no soul to continue on, and the decomposition of the body is all there is, I would never have been able to endure the death of my son.

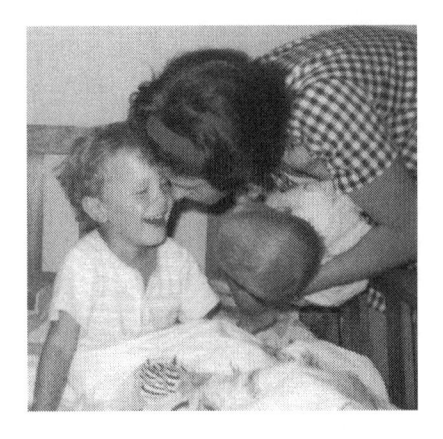

The more I believed in the transition from one world to the next, his death began to become bearable; it became easier for me to accept; it has just taken on a new form. Having said that, I will never stop longing to hug him and be hugged by him.

I now see him in empty rooms, in places where he liked to go; doing things he liked to do; imagining him as he would have looked years later. These are not tricks of the light. They are aches of the mind … longings, and I cry.

He is all around us as we look at his art work, remember his voice, his silly antics, his smiles, and recall the memories he left with us. All of what he was *is*. All of what he was is here with us. I believe he will always be with us, whether we realize it or not.

When I opened my mind and heart to the possibility that he can be here, I was filled with renewed strength.

It then became possible for me to give to my children what they have always been able to give to me … unconditional love.

"Unbeing dead isn't being alive."

e e cummings

Chapter Twenty Three
The Circle Of Life

Time … the one thing we have and don't have at all. We eventually come to the realization that something embedded in our subconscious leads us to continually search for pathways and answers in life to explore why we are here … where here is … and examine what it is we think we believe.

I am not a woman of deep religious knowledge, nor am I a scientist. Not a day goes by that I don't question what it is I believe, but I'm pretty certain that everything happens for a reason. Whether or not you choose to believe me, this book is one of them. As I began weaving a memoir of the events and people in my life, my stream of consciousness carried me out of my box through an amazing spiritual and scientific journey.

The truth is we don't really know technically if life exists after death. However, if we believe it does, we can recognize that by allowing our intellect to recede we permit our free thought to give rise to our intuition. This in turn enables us to validate through our mind's eye, a term that comes from the Zen *shengen,* that there is an eternal spiritual energy in the universe.

Baruch Spinoza, a Dutch philosopher of Sephardic-Portuguese heritage, said one short profound phrase which has remained with me ... *God is.* God is the one who created time when there was no time ... the one who created a place from a continuous flow of spiritual energy, a continuous flow of love, when there was nothing.

From the day we are born this continuous flow of energy enables us to be interconnected with the knowledge of all. We all live through everything together - a heart within a heart, not on on top of a pyramid but at the center of our life's circle, connecting us all by moving independently.

During the later years of Mama's life, she lived across the street from the beach. She would say that she felt like a useless speck of nothing in a vast ocean of waves carrying her through life wherever it chose to flow, making her feel she was not in control of her own life.

I tried to explain to her that I likened the movement of the ocean's waves to that of plying the unknown waters of my journey. They were carrying me from one expanse to another as a result of my free will and the choices I was making, consciously or unconsciously, not looking back nor looking forward. The waves would finally subside in the sand only to begin another journey, and the water would once again begin to trickle out. Life's continual renewal. The body dies; the soul lives on.

I would hope that everything is encoded in the cells of our DNA uniting us all in this large universe. Imagine how marvelous it would be to have a lineage within us that could connect us with human history and a universal intelligence. I still wonder if this is really who/what God is ... a universal intelligence.

Although we may not have memory or understanding at birth as to why and how things will happen, there is astonishing clarity of thought that comes to us when approaching death. I learned from my son that the dying let us know exactly what they need to be at peace. Our initial response is denial, which makes our biggest difficulty our ability to listen to and hear what they're saying to us.

We don't know how long of an earthly life we have before we move on. Sadly, however, we have learned that death has no age. Life is not here or there. It is here and now, heaven on earth. We are all one flow of spiritual energy in a holographic universe where we cross over in time, and life goes on.

Nothing is lost when a loved one passes. Love just takes on a different form. What differentiates us is perspective, and memory becomes our partner.

In Constantine Cavafy's poem 'Ithaka,' he wrote - *may your journey be a long one; full of adventure, full of discovery.* I may not know how long my journey will be, but I try to make it full of adventure and discovery. I believe it is necessary for us to understand the life we live on earth, what we did - how we acted and why - how we reacted and interacted - because every path we cross and every person we meet is for a reason, altering our life forever.

A timeless question is whether life on this earth is considered a beginning or an end. I would say *neither.* If we believe our soul flows throughout Eternity then life is a circle and both birth and death are similar experiences with repeating journeys throughout lifetimes.

**"The past is but the past of a beginning."
(H.G. Wells)**

When people speak of an afterlife, they think of heaven or hell. I don't believe there is a place called hell except in our minds. There are no tortures or punishment. People punish themselves by their own misbehavior and/or ignorance. Our ability to understand all that is seen and unseen lies within us, and love is our guiding principle.

I am not asking you to believe me; not a day goes by that I don't question what it is I believe. I am, however, receptive to the power of human reason called enlightenment, and I leave myself open to further knowledge.

In a visit to a medium, he asked if there would be a sign letting him know when his brother was with him. The response was that his brother would be with him when he saw large spoons. During a family gathering a reservation had been made at a restaurant where they were directed to a room with an intimate setting for the family. Upon entering his eyes fell on a wall hanging in the center of the room, a wall hanging of very large spoons. Quite amazing!

I have to believe what I have learned is true to make sense of the cards that have been dealt. Scientific research has greatly advanced over the last 35 to 50 years since those events in my life took place and impacted my life. There is so much information available now.

Unable to discern what is and what isn't, we hope revelation will come to us in our lifetime … when the time is right. Our mind is our greatest obstacle.

I wonder how our destiny would have played out, and how our lives would have changed if those events took place today? Would it have made a difference? Will my thoughts still be the same 10 years from now? Perhaps the answer is really a very simple one … that it would not have mattered at all, and we would have reached exactly where we are today. The simplest answers somehow seem to be the ones that often elude us. I leave that thought to each of you to discern.

"I think of life as a good book. The further you get into it, the more it begins to make sense."

(Harold Kushner)

*"I want to know God's thoughts;
the rest are details."*

Albert Einstein

Post Script
By The Way

I extend my heartfelt thanks to all who challenged me by saying that the things I see and feel are unrealistic. That only enhanced my efforts to try to understand what flashes upon my mind, which doesn't necessarily require reason, merely a perception that I cannot see, but I can feel.

You've heard me say throughout this book that when coincidences occur, I try not to ignore them; that these life experiences are clues to discovery; that when the time is right, things will happen. And they did. The Summer of 2014 I finally began to write on the spiritual island of Patmos, Greece, and continued on the island of Cyprus throughout the Autumn.

Our spirit knows that all lives intersect. The life of my second-born son born in August of 1966 intersected with my neighbor in Cyprus, born on the same day in August of 1966. I felt as if I'd made a complete circle. Not knowing where it would lead, my thoughts began to flow freely, the pieces of my book began to fit together, and I believed I would finally finish writing this book. Since you're reading it, I did just that.

I have an interest in numerology. I consider numerology an extension of mathematics and the language of the universe. In numerology the total number of one's birth date breaks down to a single digit. Those who fall into the number of my second son's birthdate are creative, strong, unwavering, and have a pioneering spirit.

It wasn't until I was writing this last chapter that I realized my second-born son and my daughter-in-law shared the same number. Do you find that astonishing? I also realized that my mother and my first-born son also shared the same number. Is that coincidental? Was there a message I needed to learn from them? It was their lives that propelled my passion to write this book. It was from them I learned that compassion is the key to love.

We don't come into this life with guarantees. We expect we'll have our share of struggle, some more, some less, however, there is a higher power that balances the world, and within it our lives.

Albert Einstein, theoretical physicist and philosopher of science, once said:

> *"Science without religion is lame.*
> *Religion without science is blind."*

My first-born son was a neuroscientist whose tragedy led him to become a priest. Science and religion merged, enabling him to gather insight into understanding the spiritual landscape of God and that of the universe and conveying it in his ministry.

My daughter-in-law was compassionate and loving. She played Christmas carols on the piano throughout the year, living her life with the belief that hope, peace, and love were essential to living a happy life.

The life of my second-born son filled the heart of our family with love and understanding. He was able to maintain joy and happiness in spite of his adversity, which enabled him to develop a deep sense of compassion and love for all who knew him, bringing us all happiness and peace.

Mama was a religious woman who expressed her love through her actions, always giving without expecting anything in return. She was the perfect example of kindness and gentility, a woman respected and loved by all who knew her. What better way to serve humanity.

We were all able to share these special gifts between us, and they were returned to us a hundred-fold. It was their lives and actions that taught me that love is the purpose of life.

In August 2016 my son would have been 50 years old. The light of which he spoke is ever-present in our lives, ever-present within us. If we accept what others have seen, that this light comes to us while we're crossing or have crossed over in the spirit world, we could recognize and accept that we can also interact with that same light at other times in our lives, not only in dream-like states.

When my youngest son had suffered a concussion and was in the Emergency Room, my second-born son came to him from the spirit world and told him not to worry, that it was not his time to die, and that he would be alright. His presence became known. Somehow, in some way, the presence of those who have crossed over do become known to us.

The unexpected painful events in my life led me through unconsolable grief to finding happiness. They guided me in understanding the knowledge my son left with me ... that we are all here together, and it is possible to communicate with one another.

As I was completing this last chapter I thought of all that I had written. Was it my imagination? I desperately needed to connect with my loved ones; I needed to find out if that in which I believed and about which I had written was all really true.

One afternoon I went to a medium for a session. From the moment I walked in the door I was overwhelmed with joy. I could sense loved ones waiting for me as eagerly as I was waiting to communicate with them. Greeting me were my son, my daughter-in-law, my mother, my father, my brother, the children's father, as well as numerous other loved ones with whom I was able to communicate through the medium's ability to interface with the spirit world. They knew I was writing a book and that I had deep family concerns. Without my asking they shared their messages with me; detailed and specific.

I did not have to seek further. It was evident to me that we are indeed all interconnected in this magnificent universe that transcends time and space; we are all living in the here and now and our loved ones are always with us. This was my validation.

Can you imagine a future when we as infinite beings would be able to soar through the universe and become one spirit? Can you conceive of this continuity? These thoughts are in our longings. Perhaps that's where they're meant to be until the time is right; and time, after all, is relative; reality is an illusion we have control over; and Eternity is right here, right now, in a parallel dimension. No one knows what the future will unfold.

Thank you for joining me in my journey, a journey that helped me reach a place of hope and of greater understanding beyond my human life as to what I feel yet incapable of seeing. By accepting the reality of my sadness I found peace and happiness. I hope I was able to help you open your third eye and make it possible for you to seek the pathway and beauty in life that is best for you.

> *"Do not stand at my grave and weep.*
> *I am not there; I do not sleep.*
> *Do not stop at my grave and cry.*
> *I am not there; I do not die."*

(an excerpt from an anonymous poem left by a soldier in Northern Ireland going off to war)

With memory as our partner, let us cherish those we love. They travel with us *Living In Eternity.*

Efrosini A. Pappas

I was born and raised in Brooklyn, New York, of Greek heritage. My parents were my role models, and at an early age I learned that communication with the spirit world is possible and to believe in dreams.

Living In Eternity is my first book, a process which began over 50 years ago. I believe things don't happen until they're meant to happen … and you're now reading it.

I have enjoyed a fascinating career in the Travel, Art and Entertainment industries, and as a teacher of the Greek language, culture and traditions. In 2016, I produced *Love Song To Greece,* a multi-media presentation and companion guide.

The most meaningful part of my life has been my 5 children and 12 grandchildren, the loves of my life.

Robert Frost summed up everything he learned about life in three words … *It goes on.* May your journey be long, full of discovery and adventure, and lead you to the pathway that is best for you. Keep smiling, from the inside/out.